A Video Arts Guide

So you think you can sell?

In the same series:

So you think you can manage?

Video Arts

Cartoons by Shaun Williams

So you think you can sell?

Methuen . London

First published in Great Britain 1985
by Methuen London Ltd
11 New Fetter Lane, London EC4P 4EE
© 1985 Video Arts Ltd
Illustrations © 1985 Methuen London Ltd
Printed in Great Britain

British Library Cataloguing in Publication Data

So you think you can sell? – (A Video Arts guide)
1. Selling
I. Video Arts   II. Series
658.8'5   HF5438.25

ISBN 0–413–57400–8
ISBN 0–413–57420–2 Pbk

Contents

1
So you want to be
a success at selling? *page* 9

2
Difficult customers 39

3
'When I'm calling you' –
telephone customer relations 58

4
The cold call – telephone sales 75

5
The show business 93

6
The proposal 111

7
Negotiation 122

8
It's all right,
it's only a customer 146

So you think
you can sell?

Don't apologise for yourself.

1 So you want to be a success at selling?

So you want to be a success at selling? That sounds a pretty reasonable idea; after all, who wants to be a failure? Selling successfully can lead to big rewards and a good career. But how can we help you to be a success? Well, if you are new to the sales game we will give you some ideas about how to sell to existing customers and potential clients, and, hopefully, whet your appetite for more knowledge. If you are an experienced salesperson we will remind you of all those things you already know but which 20,000 miles of motorway driving a year have slightly erased from your memory.

We have assumed, whether you are a novice or an old hand, that you know all that stuff about cleaning your car, arriving on time, making sure you haven't slept in your suit and don't have mud on your shoes (fertiliser salespeople and building site suppliers are let off that last point). This same assumption incorporates not assaulting the buyer's secretary or reversing into the Chairman's Rolls Royce in the car park. You may say, 'I wish I had reversed into it, it's the nearest I'll ever get to one.' That is what this book is really all about. It's about making you change your approach from thinking small to thinking big. You too will be driving a Rolls Royce when you really are a success at selling.

We are going to begin by thinking about the sales interview itself, since this is after all the heart of the matter. We'll look at how you should conduct the interview, from the initial research to closing the deal. You probably think research sounds very boring. After all, you want to be out there in the field fighting the good fight with customers, not sitting in an office drowning in statistics, computer print-outs and reference books. But like any good warrior, when you are selling you need to be prepared for the battle to come – to have worked out a strategy, thought through

How do you see yourself?

Never say, think or believe 'I'm just a rep' or even 'just a sales manager'. Your customer will probably never meet your seniors. To him you are your company – he is talking to it through you. If your company is good, he will have a respect for it that you can benefit from. And it is good, isn't it . . . really? So don't apologise for yourself: after all, you are Mr ABC Computers, or Miss XYZ Muckshifters.

what the enemy might do, how he might counter-attack, how you can use your weapons and armaments to their best abilities. So that is what research is all about – not hours of studying dry tomes but providing a background in the key areas of your sales approach:

Research the customer
Research the product
Research the relationship

'Oh,' you are saying, 'that sort of research – I do all that. I know most of my customers, I've been selling this stuff for ages and there is nothing I do not know about their relationships!'

But wait a minute. Before being so dismissive take a closer look at each of these three areas.

It's amazing how details fade over the period since the last sales call. Much as all of us salespeople are inclined to believe that our customers and their personal habits, likes and dislikes are printed in indelible ink on our brains, it is very easy to forget and get people muddled. This can have embarrassing consequences. Let's take a look at what happened to one sales rep who hadn't done his homework.

Salesperson: Nice to see you again, Mr Jennings.
Customer: Jenkins.
Salesperson: How's Mrs Jenkins keeping?
Customer: I haven't the faintest idea what's happened to her since our marriage broke up.
Salesperson: Oh dear, I'm sorry about that.
Customer: Well, at least you're consistent. You were sorry the last two times I told you as well.

So before you meet your customer, you must

find out all you can about his personal circumstances. Get his name right. Whether he's married. How many children, their names. His hobbies. Or the fact that he doesn't like to spend valuable office time talking about his wife, his children and his hobbies.

Of course this is only one aspect of researching the customer. There are plenty of others. What about researching him and his position in the company? Just because life seems one continuous round of non-events and repeat performances for you – if it's Monday, it's Leeds, and if it's Tuesday, its Bradford – it doesn't mean that the customer's world has stood still. But it's very easy to make that assumption and fall into the traps it inevitably creates:

Salesperson: This is one of our new binding machines. Very compact. Very light. Easy to carry. Twenty-eight per cent faster but only five per cent more expensive. And they come in nine different colours.

Customer: Very nice, but you realise that since our reorganisation I no longer have authority to buy them. Our Mr Willoughby authorises the buying now.

Salesperson: What? And you let me cart this all the way up here? These things weigh a ton. I might have guessed you'd gone down in the world! Tiny cubbyhole of an office. Only a three-peg hat stand.

Customer: But of course Mr Willoughby's decision invariably reflects the advice I give him . . .

So, you have to research not only your customer himself, but also his position in the firm's structure. Of course you also have to make sure that you understand how his business works:

Research the customer

This means not only remembering his name, but keeping abreast with his position in the firm. Possibly the person you deal with has been promoted. In that case make sure if you can that he introduces you to his successor. That means that the relationship you developed originally gets 'handed down' to the new customer and you have a head start. But never fall into the trap of saying 'Oh, Mr So-and-So always bought that range.' You need to build a new relationship, taking advantage of the old, and you don't do this by destroying the new one on day one.

Researching the customer also means knowing about his business. Try to think of your product as a benefit – specifically for the customer. You need him, but he also needs you. The more authority you can bring to establishing this relationship the more sales will result.

But the customer is, of course, to be seen as part of the business he is in. See what you can learn about that business from the trade press, advertising, his catalogues, his competition etc, so that you identify with his job as well as yours.

Salesperson: We've got a new range of delicious pies. I know you've got pies already, but not like these. Veal and mushroom, pork and orange, rabbit and prune, lamb and passion fruit. Turn your shop into a gourmet's paradise!

Customer: But . . .

Salesperson: I know, I know. You haven't got the storage facilities to keep them warm without drying them up. That's no problem with our microwave multi-storage cabinet.

Customer: We are a high-class bakery. We make our own pies. Our clientèle wouldn't dream of buying convenience foods. If you'll excuse me . . .

It's your business to find out about their business. You should keep full records and check them. Some organisations have a very high profile. They are constantly written about in the trade press, they regularly advertise and produce reports for their employees which they scatter in reception for visitors such as you and me to read and take away. A regular read of the trade press, the business press, and maybe even a switch of television channels from a soap opera to a science or current affairs programme could stand you in good stead and give you more knowledge of your market place, your customers and their competitors.

You don't need to have won Mastermind to be able to sell, but a little knowledge, coupled of course with flair and persuasive skills, goes a long way to making you a success story. Did you notice that word 'knowledge'? It leads us neatly into the area of **Product Knowledge**. It is the next key aspect of research.

Know your own strengths and weaknesses

All-round perfect salespeople only exist in textbooks. Some people can be flummoxed by fast talk with figures. Others have an extreme aversion to using that helpful object, the telephone. Some people have bad memories. Others excel in these areas but can't spell. You should know your strengths and lead with them. You should know your weaknesses and protect them. Don't hide them. It's better to say you are easily thrown by figures – let's take it through slowly. Do your best to overcome your weaknesses if they are not inborn.

Have you ever been caught out or bowled middle stump by a customer who seems to know more about your product or service and its application than you do? Very tricky. Or perhaps your problem lies in keeping abreast of all those new products that pour off your production line, or are brought in from far-flung points of the globe . . .

Salesperson: I understand that you're now buying for both toys and electrical goods.

Customer: Absolutely correct.

Salesperson: And you've now got an improved computerised system, so that you have to place your Christmas orders in May?

Customer: Another bullseye! You're well informed.

Salesperson: I make it my business to be.

Customer: I'll tell you what I'm really interested in. Your new electronic high-speed drills.

Salesperson: Yes, well, they are new . . . so new that I haven't got the literature.

Customer: I'm sure you can tell me all about them, though.

Salesperson: Oh yes. They're nice, actually. Very nice.

Customer: Remote-controlled, are they? Drill-a-hole-from-the-comfort-of-your-armchair type of touch?

Salesperson: I think so. Or was that the modern space satellite? Anyway, they come in, er, several different colours. Well, at least one different colour.

Customer: Good day.

You see? Customer research is only half of it. You've also got to research the product. You won't be able to sell what you don't know about. So why not take some time to find out? Suggest to your sales manager that he breaks the habit of centuries and at the next sales meeting talks about the new products and their applications rather than discuss the

Research the product

Nobody in Sales ever lost their job by badgering their manager for more information. The literature about new and existing products, relevant facts about improvements in the pipeline, new ranges about to be introduced and so on are not state secrets – they are the tools of *your* trade.

In sales training courses one of the most basic exercises is 'overcoming objections'. This consists of one sales rep raising every objection he can think of, addressing himself to another rep. This 'game' is equally useful to both parties, and can be played at any sales conference without the need to do it at expensive residential courses. The objector, of course, must use it to ask the questions he or she fears most. Many of them will involve 'product knowledge' and must be repeated until a satisfactory answer is reached, for everyone's benefit!

boring old sales statistics which, as we all know, can be contrived to prove anything.

Although it is no substitute for the salesman's knowledge, sales literature can be an invaluable back-up. But remember, the buyer will find it awfully difficult to concentrate if you hand him a brochure to read and continue to talk. He will get confused. Is he supposed to read or listen? So give him a chance to glance through it in peace and only carry on talking when he seems to have finished looking at the brochure.

Of course it is not enough to research your product – you also have to know what your company is capable of.

Salesperson: This is the only lawnmower in the world with a brain – the electric sensor adjusts the cutting edges to deal with thick grass, thin grass, weeds and so on.

Customer: Very impressive. What about delivery dates?

Salesperson: Oh definitely.

Customer: You can give me delivery dates?

Salesperson: Absolutely.

Customer: Well, when?

Salesperson: Er – next Tuesday?

Customer: I can have two dozen machines by next Tuesday?

Salesperson: No, you can have the delivery dates next Tuesday.

Customer: I see. What about repairs and spares?

Salesperson: These things never break down. Hardly ever.

Customer: But if they do, what sort of service will I get?

Salesperson: Don't ask me, I'm not the service department, am I?

So you need to have done your research about the customer and his firm, and about the product and your firm.

Finally, you must look into what has happened in your firm's previous dealings with the customer – the layers of fact and fiction which make up **the history of the relationship** between your two organisations. Anyone who has just taken over a sales territory and is struggling with the problem of non-existent or out-of-date records will understand that knowing the history of dealings with a customer can save time, embarrassment and hassle. (So fill in your records – don't inflict this agony on your successor.)

By the way, assuming that there are no computerised records available to you and that you are trying to fight your way out of this sort of muddle, customer accounts departments can be a useful source of information on past relationships with a customer. They often have the whole saga on a client and have a picture of the dealings which have taken place. This is because they are the ones who have to bear the brunt of a client refusing to pay, not paying in full or delaying payment because of some form of inefficiency on the part of your company. It may take some time for customer accounts to sort out their information but if all other sources of information are fruitless, why not chat up a member of your accounts staff?

But for the rest of us, dealing in established territories with customers we know, it is awfully easy to adopt the attitude that our job is done once we have taken the order. After all, there is a perfectly good sales office – living off our toil – to support us back at base. That approach can lead to scenes such as this:

Salesperson: Last time you ordered
twelve dozen. Shall we say fifteen dozen
this time?
Customer: I haven't had the twelve dozen
yet.
Customer: Still? I could have sworn I saw
one of our lorries here when I passed
last week.
Customer: You did. They were delivering
the modified versions of the ten dozen
we ordered before the twelve dozen and
which we sent back because you hadn't
made the modifications which you said
you'd made before you sent them in the
first place.
Salesperson: Ah, I didn't know about
that . . .

So, before hitting the trail, find out what
happened to the customer's last order – did it
go through on time, was it satisfactory? Also
check to see whether he has placed any direct
business through telephone sales in the
interim. You will feel so much more assured
and seem so much more on the ball to the
client if you have all the facts at your
fingertips and are in a position to defuse
rather than react to situations. Information
breeds confidence. Confidence breeds success.

'I was just passing,
    so I thought I'd drop in.'
'Saw your car outside,
    so I thought I'd say hello.'

You know the sort of character who makes
these remarks? The missionless salesman
who wanders hither and thither, to wherever
he know's there'll be a warm welcome, a
comfy chair and a cup of coffee. 'That's a bit
hard,' you're saying, 'some of my colleagues
use those phrases and they don't do so
badly.' Perhaps. But the point is that they and

you would do better if all sales calls had a purpose – an objective. By the way, a cosy chat and a warm office may be nice on a cold winter's day, but it is not an objective. Dropping in on a customer without an objective is like doing the week's shopping without a shopping list – just wandering around, hoping for inspiration.

Customer: Well, you really seem to understand our problems.
Salesperson: That's my business, you know.
Customer: You always make me feel better. I really enjoy our little chats.
Salesperson: Oh, I'm glad. So do I.
Customer: I wish I didn't have to rush off, but I have to go and see that fellow that keeps selling me things.
Salesperson: Yes, I know the type . . .

Your objective must be realistic, and it must incorporate some alternatives. If you are selling paper clips a reasonable objective may be a sale of, say, 10,000 clips in a call. If you are selling a new product line of groceries your original objective may be to sell four cases, though your alternatives could include a sale of fewer cases, then one case, then one case on sale or return. This one case on sale or return could be your final fall-back position. Of course, if you are selling highly technical, one-off items such as advanced computer systems or nuclear generators you are not likely to get a buying decision from one call.

Salesperson: We could provide your sixty-three branches with a fully integrated computer system linked to the main-frame CPU in your head office in London. All right? That's all your records, payments, internal communications fully automatic within

List your aims and aids

When you walk out of this call, what do you hope to have achieved? Fix it in your mind before you go in. It may be only to set up a friendly relationship, but that's not selling. It may be to close a large sale, or to rescue a disastrous situation caused by bad service. Prepare for it. Note your aims. Note your aids – product benefits, service improvements; work out how you will introduce these points in the face of a customer's objections.

five years, and it comes in nine different colours.

Customer: Mind-boggling.

Salesperson: Exactly. So will you have a couple?

Customer: Well I'd hardly need more than one, would I?

Salesperson: OK, one it is. I'll send the invoice.

Customer: Hang on! I can't order a computer system costing millions of pounds just like that.

Salesperson: You mean you're not actually going to buy one? Oh Christ!

Your objective doesn't have to be a sale every time. Sometimes something much less is the most you can hope for, like an assurance that the customer's Board will hire a firm of consultants to do a full cost-benefit study of your proposed system.

So you need an objective – to get an order or a commitment to a survey, or whatever, and you need some alternatives prepared. There are a couple of other aspects to this objective-setting area – they involve a bit of lateral thinking! It is awfully easy to get stuck in the groove – to think that what the customer bought or expressed an interest in at the last meeting is the sum total of what he needs to buy through you. But ask yourself what else he has the responsibility to buy. What other products or services might his company require? Better still, ask him! If you don't ask, your competitors certainly will and the chances are that they will get the business.

Many organisations – however small or large – have split the buying responsibility. For instance, the managing director's secretary may buy the stationery while someone else buys the print, or the transport manager buys fleet cars and trucks while the company secretary buys the executives' cars. So why not ask who else could be interested – the answer may lead to bigger, better orders than any you could negotiate with your existing contact, whose part in the operation is worthwhile but small.

Salesperson: Presumably you'll want to re-order the same items you had last time?

Customer: No. We're not using those drugs any more.

Salesperson: I'd have thought you'd need more now you've opened your new surgical department in Brick Street.

Customer: Brick Street buy all their own supplies.

Salesperson: Ah! Who should I contact over in Brick Street, then?

Customer: Miss Lewis.

Salesperson: Why are you needing fewer drugs?

Customer: Because we're using fewer drugs.

Salesperson: Any particular reason?

Customer: Our policy has changed. We're using new techniques.

Salesperson: What new techniques?

Customer: We're using plastic parts. Instead of treating the affected part, it's often better to whip it out and replace it.

Salesperson: But we sell plastic parts. And you'll need our tissue compatibility drugs too, presumably?

By the way, if your customer gives you the name of someone else in the organisation who could be interested in the product or service you are selling, do remember to thank him for the contact and to involve him in the approach. Don't appear to drop him just because you smell a bigger fish in another area of the organisation. In the words of the old saying, be nice to people on the way up, you may meet them again on the way down.

So, **set objectives**. Have a clear objective, but prepare alternatives and fallbacks. Then look for other customers for your product, and finally look for other products for your customer.

After all this research and objective-setting you are now probably more than ready for a face-to-face chat with the customer – to make a sale. But before you rush off and put these points into practice, do remember the magic phrase, 'ask questions'. Actually, it would be better to say, 'ask open questions' – ones which don't demand the answer 'yes' or 'no', then you will avoid some of those wonderfully monosyllabic sales conversations which go nowhere and gradually freeze up. You know the sort of thing:

Salesperson: So, are you going to buy one?
Customer: No.
Salesperson: You mean . . . no?
Customer: Yes.
Salesperson: Definitely not?
Customer: Definitely not.
Salesperson: So would I be right in thinking that you are not, in fact, going to have any?
Customer: Yes.
Salesperson: Well, that's all my questions. Thank you for being so . . . frank.

No, you must ask open questions, ones that don't demand the answer 'yes' or 'no'. You must ask what, who, where, when and how. 'Why?' can sound aggressive or impertinent. It's better to ask for the reason:

Salesperson: Any particular reason?
Customer: Yes.
Salesperson: May I ask what it is?

Customer: New policy. We don't buy that
sort of equipment any more. We hire it.
Salesperson: So you might be interested
in hiring some?
Customer: Yes, but your company
doesn't hire.
Salesperson: We do now, since January.
Customer: Oh, well in that case . . .

Let's have another look at how open-ended
questions help you gain information:

Salesperson: So would you be interested
in buying advertising space in our
publication?
Customer: What's the circulation?
Salesperson: How important is the size
of the circulation?
Customer: Very. Why does anyone
advertise? I want people to read it.
Salesperson: What sort of people?
Customer: The influential people in the
industry.
Salesperson: So it's the quality of
readership you're after, really, not just
the size of the circulation?
Customer: Yes, I suppose I am.

So the use of open-ended questions does
two things for you:

1 It gives you vital current information about
the client, his thinking, his needs and his
future plans.
2 It involves him in the conversation.

Once he has been drawn into the conversation by the use of this technique, the
customer is quite likely to relax a little (and
tell more) because you have involved him and
in a sense are expressing an interest in him
and his business. No one likes being talked
at, and this type of question makes him feel at
least partially in control. That is a potential

21

Technique

The good salesperson has more technique than a concert pianist. It's one of the charms and challenges of your job, to cope with varied and unexpected situations. As we show, most customers conform to types. So do most salespeople. Don't be afraid to be a little surprising – not by having an electric bow-tie but by thinking how you can be different yet still communicate effectively. What would you prefer to be – 'old so-and-so from Parker's' or 'that chap from Parker's – he's always got an interesting view on things'. You can do this by anticipating objections and planning answers that are open questions themselves. This throws the onus back on the customer.

danger – do ensure that he doesn't take control by countering your open questions with ones of his own.

Salesperson: So what sort of advertising space would you be interested in buying?
Customer: What's the circulation of your publication?
Salesperson: About 12,000.
Customer: Only 12,000?
Salesperson: Sometimes a bit more. Last month it was 12,372.
Customer: So what does that make the cost per thousand for a full page?
Salesperson: Fifty pounds.
Customer: It's not worth it.

How can you avoid this happening? Just counter his questions with your own.

Customer: Our Finance Committee has decided to centralise all the word-processing.
Salesperson: So you may need new equipment for that?
Customer: Yes, but not yours. I've had some unhappy experiences with your firm.
Salesperson: Well, two instances of late delivery of software, and one defective printer, which we replaced pretty swiftly, and none of this in the last three years since we reorganised our customer services. All our deliveries are within four weeks.
Customer: Fair enough. But I know your range, and it's not what I'm looking for.
Salesperson: Well, we've got a lot of new kit. I mean – I don't expect you to buy without seeing it, but why don't you let me lay on a tour of the factory for you?
Customer: What kind of stuff would you be thinking of showing me?

Salesperson: What kind of equipment
would you be looking for?
Customer: Not what you make.
Salesperson: All right, what then?
Customer: Small, lightweight, highly
mobile systems.
Salesperson: Well, one of my main
reasons for coming to see you today is
to tell you that we have developed a
whole range of lightweight, highly
mobile equipment. The official launch
is next month.
Customer: Why the sudden change?
Salesperson: Why your sudden change?
Customer: Because it's our business to
spot future trends before they happen.
Salesperson: Well, that's our business
too.

By using this technique, you keep control,
gain information and set yourself on a steady
course towards achieving your sales objective. In other words, the use of open
questions gives you a launching pad, to make
your presentation.

You are now ready to start selling.
First, of course, you will present your case
to the customer. Having done all your
preparation, you have now got a good picture
of his needs, aspirations and problems. So
this is your golden opportunity to explain
how your product or service will help him.
The trouble is, what seems in theory such an
easy thing to do, so often goes wrong.

Salesperson: It works by electronic
differential reading, with an anamorphic
lens and dual built-in optical refraction
correctors plus zero-parallax facility . . .
Customer: I only want clean photocopies.

23

Our pickaxes and shovels have a matching motif.

Describe the product in terms of benefits, not features.

Yes, you spotted the deliberate mistake. The salesperson described the product in terms of features as opposed to describing what those features could mean or do for the customer – in other words, the benefits. It doesn't matter how amazing the features are, or how technical the customer is – he still needs to know what the product can do for *him* and how it will meet *his* needs. The trouble is that all salespeople become very familiar with their product and its technical specifications. They sometimes find it difficult to appreciate that the customer is less 'turned on' by all the technical trickery. It is too easy to use familiar product or company jargon when presenting to customers. But features do not sell products, benefits do. Suppose a surgeon described an operation to a patient purely in terms of its amazing features:

Surgeon: Have I got the operation for you! Only three incisions, an Anderson slash, a Ridgeways sideways double fillet and a standard dormer slit, five minutes with the scalpel top whack, only thirty stitches. We can take out up to five pounds of your insides and have you back in your hospital bed in seventy-five minutes flat. And we can do ten in a day. Shall I put you down for three?

Patient: I don't want three, I don't want one. I don't need it.

Surgeon: Fair enough. Here's a better one. Only just in – the very latest. Right? We bore two small holes in the top of your head.

Patient: No!

Surgeon: It's clever stuff, it's the very latest.

Patient: It'll hurt.

Surgeon: You'll be spark out.

Patient: What about afterwards?

Surgeon: Afterwards? Oh, I'll just have a cup of tea and be ready for the next one.

The surgeon was looking at the whole thing from his own point of view. You've got to look at what you're selling through the customer's eyes, and think about the benefits he'll receive . . .

Surgeon: The operation will relieve the pain completely. It will be a bit sore for four or five days, but within a fortnight you'll be home. You'll be able to do light gardening, go for walks, and in four weeks you'll be back at work

Patient: I understand.

The patient still may not like the thought of the operation, but with the second surgeon at least he knows what it will do for him.

He doesn't need you (he thinks)

You sell toilet paper. A company needs only one supplier. Possibly four salespeople a week try to contact the relevant buyer, who's already quite happy with the bumf provided. *He doesn't want to buy from you.* Many so-called buyers are in this position (see p. 35). And yet he needs to purchase regularly. This customer may have the dickens of a job trying to keep all the company toilets stocked. Can you ease his life by offering an extra-large roll, or a multi-roll dispenser? Suddenly you'll be on the inside track, not because your paper is necessarily better. But you, or someone, has thought about associated benefits and how to sell them. And suddenly the case of 'buyer's block' is cured.

Similarly, our customer may not like parting with his money, but at least if a product is explained in terms of benefits, he knows what he is getting for his money and can assess the value. So talk in terms of customer's needs. For instance:

Salesperson: I think you'll find the RB186 is what you need.
Customer: But that only does four copies a minute. The other does six.
Salesperson: But speed isn't vital for you, is it? As you said yourself, your reputation is for high-quality precision engineering, and you don't want to spoil that image with cheap-looking photocopies of specifications and proposals, do you? With faster copies there's always the danger you'll sacrifice quality for speed.

Of course, explaining the benefits to the customer is usually only the beginning of the selling conversation. Customers have an infuriating habit of raising objections. Dealing with these objections is an important skill for salespeople. Customers raise difficulties to play games with unskilled salespeople. They also use them as a way of expressing interest in a deal. 'I am not sure this is the right product for us,' can be translated to read, 'I don't quite understand how this product fits my needs – tell me more.'

So instead of packing up shop when you next hear:

'It's too expensive'

'It's not the right time of year for us to stock this product'

'Your deliveries are not reliable enough'

'We couldn't possibly deal through you'

'Your machines will not give us the tolerance we require'

stay in, fighting. Not literally fighting, of

course, otherwise the conversation will degenerate into this type of shouting match.

Customer: They're too expensive.
Salesperson: No they're not. They're the same price range as the competition.
Customer: I meant they're too expensive for me.
Salesperson: Why didn't you say so? We make cheaper ones.
Customer: Are they as good?
Salesperson: Of course not. They're cheaper, aren't they?
Customer: I don't want inferior ones.
Salesperson: Well, have the good ones then.
Customer: They're too expensive.
Salesperson: Stupid git!

Turn-downs and objections are not a criticism of you as a person, but are to do with the way your client sees your products. A turn-down is not a personal slight.

Customer: I'm afraid they aren't suitable.
Salesperson: I see. I'm sorry, I'm a fool.
Customer: What?
Salesperson: If I try to sell you something that isn't suitable, I must be a fool.
Customer: That isn't true.
Salesperson: You think I can't face the truth, you think I'm weak.
Customer: I just don't like them.
Salesperson: It's me you don't like. Admit it.

Apart from staying cool and not taking the objection personally, what else can you do to cope with objections? First, try to probe the reasons behind the objection, using (once again) open questions, and then attempt to make the objection specific rather than general.

Objections

Objections are opportunities. Counter them with structured questions needing more than a yes or a no. Make sure the objection is specific. Many of them can be anticipated and planned for: use your knowledge of your product and its services.

If you get a totally new and unforeseen objection, play for time whilst you compare it against what you have to offer. Objections are often thrown at you as a personal test, especially by a new customer. Play it cool, don't get rattled, and don't try to outsmart this type of customer.

Customer: In any case, I don't think your cameras are very suitable for our requirements.

Salesperson: In what way?

Customer: Well, they aren't too good for aerial photography. They vibrate too much.

Salesperson: Don't you actually mean that the plane vibrates too much, and this shakes the cameras?

Customer: I suppose I do.

Salesperson: In that case you need our new vibro-mounting.

Customer: Won't that push the cost up?

Salesperson: Yes, but it'll extend the life of the camera enormously, so in the long run it'll save you money.

Customer: How much will it save us?

Salesperson: Seventeen thousand pounds over five years.

Customer: How do you work that out?

Salesperson: I made it up.

That was good, to start with. By getting the customer to make his complaint specific the salesman managed to deal with it and even make an additional sale. Then he spoilt it all. You should alway be honest, and never bluff your way out of a hole. But if you have to make a concession, put it in perspective and always follow it with a compensation.

Customer: These electric vans are pretty slow.

Salesperson: Yes, but local delivery vans don't often get the chance to go that fast, do they?

Customer: True.

Salesperson: What we've done is to put the emphasis on economy and reliability rather than sporty performance. We've found that in these days of high transport costs, most people think that important. And, of course, it means fewer accidents, fewer prosecutions and a lot less damage to the goods inside.

So – play it cool, put the objection into perspective and point out the compensating factors.

There are other factors to bear in mind as well. The majority of sales objections do not arrive out of the great blue yonder – they are often predictable. Or put it this way; the well prepared and informed salesperson should have a fairly clear idea of the likely objections the client will raise. How? Well, from analysing his buyer over a number of calls you can usually anticipate and forestall likely trouble spots.

Of course there will be occasions when the client will, in the end, turn you down. Sometimes, for instance, he will be unable to afford the item no matter how hard you attempt to justify the price and demonstrate the resultant cost savings. So should you stay locked in battle? No, accept defeat gracefully. Remain the sort of person he'll be happy to see again. Write the situation down to experience and the laws of probability and move on to the next. By all means continue visiting the client but perhaps not with the same frequency unless other sales possibilities still exist. By keeping in touch you will be well placed to do business if and when the client's position alters.

A few buyers will raise objections with the malicious intention of putting you through your paces and seeing you sweat a bit for the order. But the main reasons why people raise objections are as follows:

1 As a smoke screen or trap for the unwary.
2 As a means of seeking more information.
3 To avoid/delay taking a decision.
4 To brief themselves for objections they themselves will meet when they recommend your product or service to their boss

29

or their colleagues.

5 Because they find it difficult to say 'no' outright and wish to let you down lightly.

If we discount the fifth of these and concentrate on the first four, you will realise that they show that clients raise objections from two main motives:

1 To mislead (reasons 1 and 3 in our list).
2 Because his objection is genuine and he needs further clarification and information (reasons 2 and 4).

Assuming that this is a fair premise – and it is one that has stood many a successful salesperson in good stead – all objections, of whatever nature, need to be looked at in a new light. In other words, before attempting to answer objections such as:

'I don't need one'
'I can't afford it'
'It'll mean too much disruption'
'Your back-up service is weak'
'I'll need to talk to others first'
you'll need to apply a few tests to make sure that you are not being led up the garden path. What are these tests? Well, fast footwork or avoiding-techniques are the order of the day. Use phrases such as:

'Leaving price aside for the moment . . .'
'What else, if anything, is troubling you?'
'Let's assume our back-up service matches that of the competition, what then?'
'If delivery wasn't a problem how would you then view this proposal?'
'Suppose this were your decision alone, would you wish to proceed with the contract?'

These are the keys to testing and avoiding false objections. What you are doing is asking the client to put his initial objection to one

The truth, the whole truth . . .

The professional salesperson is out to sell his products. All products have their benefits, and he will know his. Most products are open to some form of objection. The salesman will know these and how to counter them. But never go beyond the truth. If 2 per cent of the bottles you sell break, don't say none of them break. Find out why they break, and what's being done about it. Then you can say 'We did have a problem, but . . .' or 'I can confidently say the next batch will be intensively stress-tested.' There's no reason to bare your breast and go through all your product's defects, but you must never mislead the customer. That's not selling, it's deception.

side for the moment, then probing to see if anything else is hiding behind it. If there is another objection, this technique causes it to be revealed, and the first objection can then be ignored. You should then proceed to meet and deal with the new objection. If the initial objection is restated, then you know that it is for real and needs to be put into perspective and answered if a sale is to be made.

Let's take a look at a salesman trying to cope with the objections of a potential client.

Salesperson: Could I just ask you what makes you think this isn't the Pension Plan you're looking for?

Customer: The premiums are rather high.

Salesperson: Well, they're geared to the level of benefits you asked us to work to.

Customer: I didn't realise we'd end up paying all this.

Salesperson: But when you think that it gives every employee two-thirds of his final salary on retirement . . .

Customer: I was thinking of the cost to the company. On your scheme we do seem to contribute an excessive proportion of the total.

Salesperson: It may look like that on the face of it. But if you look here in our booklet, you'll see that after full relief on your contributions at the upper level of Corporation Tax, the real company contribution is substantially lower.

Customer: Still, I'm not happy about there being no provision for the widow or widower of an employee who dies after retirement.

Salesperson: We can easily build that in.

Customer: At an extra cost.

Salesperson: But it would be more than covered by that saving in Corporation Tax.

This scene might have looked discouraging for the salesman, but the objections showed that the customer was interested. Remember that customers may raise objections because they are, in a sense, middle men, and are going to have to take your sales proposal to a meeting and suffer a grilling on the terms and conditions, the suitability and benefits. So they use their interview with you as a dry run for this.

Look at the scene that followed our last interview, one that the salesman never normally sees.

1st Colleague: The premiums are pretty steep, aren't they?

Customer: They're geared to the level of benefit we asked them to work to.

1st Colleague: Even so, it's a pretty hefty whack.

Customer: Still, if we want to give every employee two-thirds of his final salary on retirement, we can't do it for nothing.

2nd Colleague: It's not the total amount so much. It's the enormous proportion that the company has to pay.

Customer: But if you take off the tax relief the company gets, it's nothing like so big.

By the way, salespeople often invite the price objection because they leave the price as a bald statement. 'It will cost £10,000.' They don't surround the price with benefits to soften the blow. Also, salespeople are inclined to deal in total and not in unit costs. The best way of presenting price is always to present the total cost and then the unit cost, but always surround this pricing with benefits, so it becomes a sandwich: 'The price to include delivery will be £100 at a unit price of 10 pence per reinforced bolt.'

We have mentioned a number of techniques that you can use in objection handling. There are a number of others, including the **Pre-Emptive Strike Technique.**

Why not play the buyer at his own game? So you have been calling on Mr Hard-to-Budge for a few months. He buys a number of your products, but not at the more expensive end of your range as he claims his clientèle are not the right types for these items. Try building his objection into your initial sales approach at the next meeting.

'Well, I know there is no point in discussing the premium range because your clientèle wouldn't be right for this merchandise.' By building this into your sales presentation you will provoke two main reactions:

1 You rob the buyer of his 'pet' objection – so now he is off his guard.
2 A contradiction. Because you have said it, and you are the salesperson he may feel obliged to contradict you.

Either way, you have now created an opening for yourself.

Another technique that can be useful in handling objections is **Agreeing.**

This is always disarming. The buyer raises an objection and before he knows where he is he hears you, the salesman, agreeing with him. But of course, you don't stop at the point of agreement, you go on to point out the reasons why.

So if the buyer says:

'You're more expensive than the competition'

'You don't give dealers promotion support' or

'You don't deal on a sale-or-return basis' try the agreement with reason technique. That is, of course, if there are valid reasons why your products are more expensive or you don't offer the other types of service mentioned above. Go ahead, agree with the buyer, and then go on to point out why and what in the long term this can mean to the buyer. In other words, state the benefits.

Well, now. We've enthused the customer with the benefits and met and overcome his objections. Now we just need to wait for him to place the order. But why wait for him? Why not ask for the order? It may not be very British, nor even seem very polite to ask for things, but it's amazing how many more orders we would all get if we either asked for the order or listened out for the customer giving us the buying signal. Such remarks as . . .

'Well, they look very much the kind of thing we're looking for.'

'They really do look good.'

'They're not cheap – but I suppose that nothing that's any good is cheap.'

So, of course, you can close the sale on a buying signal, using one of many 'closing-the-sale techniques' which often rejoice in lovely names like 'the puppy-dog close', the 'Benjamin Franklin close', the 'Balance-sheet close'. Be sophisticated if you like, but the plain old assumptive technique:

'So we'll put you down for four cases?'

'So you'll join our list of stockists?'

or the well tried and proven 'alternative' technique:

'Would you like 10,000 or 20,000?'

'Would you like deliveries to start this week or next?'

have helped to boost many a salesperson's bonus. By the way, when using the alternative close, leave the choice you would prefer the customer to make as a second option – 10,000 or 20,000. This way you are encouraging positive thought.

One last point. Having closed the sale, SHUT UP. The chances are that if you don't, you will talk yourself out of the order. This often happens, so do be careful.

Salesperson: And here at last is an elegant shoe that will last.

Customer: I must say that's what a lot of our customers complain they can't get. The price is very reasonable.

Salesperson: So you'll join our list of stockists?

Customer: Yes, I certainly will.

Salesperson: Excellent, marvellous, terrific. Well, if you send in the completed order form very quickly, that'll avoid delays at the factory.

Customer: Oh. Do you have delays at the factory?

Salesperson: No, no. the effects of the last strike are pretty minimal now.

Customer: I think maybe I ought to think this over.

You see? If he had just kept quiet everything would have been all right.

Now, let's follow a sale through from beginning to end. Our unfortunate salesman is visiting old Arkwright, a chemist. If he can sell to Arkwright, he can sell to anyone.

Customer: What is it? I've got better things to do than listen to salesmen blathering on about products I don't want.

Salesperson: That's all right, Mr Arkwright, I'm only here to blather on about products you do want.

Customer: I've got too much already. It's customers I'm short of, not stock.

Salesperson: So that means you want something that's going to move fast?

Customer: What, the cheap stuff? I don't sell that kind of rubbish. My customers come here for quality merchandise.

Salesperson: I was thinking of our new range of perfume.

Close confidently

Read the signals. Buying can be a big decision and many buyers are nervous, others just inarticulate. Here you have to be very alert and sensitive. Don't worry about elaborate closing techniques. Like sex manuals, they need joint participation and you haven't got that. Common sense is the best guide here, if you have correctly assessed your customer. But don't be hesitant. This is the stage where the matter-of-fact approach is most likely to win the day. And when it's done, relax. Don't rush out to scream with triumph in the car park. You and he, or she, have done a deal that should make sense for both and pave the way for a fruitful return visit. Find a compliment that isn't a tired cliché. 'It's a pleasure to do business with you,' carries little conviction. 'I'm really glad you raised that point about the grommets . . .' can lead to the customer and yourself both feeling that it's been a real meeting of minds.

I know you'll be happy with our product –
I can't think why the trade press slagged it off . . .

Having closed the sale, shut up.

Customer: What's it called?

Salesperson: It's modern, fresh, lively. Looks as if it could become quite a cult among the young. It's called 'Lover'.

Customer: Disgusting.

Salesperson: I know what you mean, but the independent market research we commissioned shows that everyone seems to like it. It could be the fast-moving line you're looking for.

Customer: Not my kind of merchandise at all.

Salesperson: Any special reason?

Customer: We don't get young people in here. They go to the chainstores and supermarkets.

Salesperson: Yes, but it's only one younger perfume you'd be stocking, and fifty for older people, and you want younger people's business, don't you?

Customer: But we don't stock a young range at all. They don't come in here.

Salesperson: But older people buy presents for younger people, don't they? And if youngsters know you stock this, that could bring them in and introduce them to your other quality merchandise, as their taste becomes sophisticated.

Customer: Yes, young people are fickle. One shop today, another one tomorrow, they've got no sense of loyalty.

Salesperson: That's true. Still, they're the ones with the spending power nowadays, aren't they?

Customer: Oh aye. Damn sight more money than's good for them. And more than they know what to do with.

Salesperson: So shall I put you down for a case?

Customer: Half a case.

Salesperson: As you like. But there's an extra two per cent discount on a case for first-time orders.

Customer: All right, but it'd better move if you want to come back here again.

Golden rules

Do research: research the customer; research the product; research the relationship.

Set objectives: prepare alternatives; find other customers for the product; find other products for the customer.

Ask questions: ask open questions; keep control.

Explain the benefits: benefits not features; customer's needs.

Meet objections: play it cool; make it specific; put it in perspective; follow it with a compensation.

Close the sale: watch for buying signals; ask for the order; keep your mouth shut.

We have considered how you should prepare for a sales interview, and how you should carry it through. We are now going to look in detail at some of the awkward characters you may encounter when you are selling . . . the ones who just *won't* say yes when presented with a sales proposal. We have divided them into **Duckers**, **Ditherers** and **Dictators**, and most buyers fit into one of these categories.

However, before we look at how the personality and style of the buyer may affect the selling process, we have to ask whether the buyer is a 'professional' or 'technical' buyer.

The professional buyer is someone who has the word 'buyer' or some such in his job title. So he is someone who spends his life buying goods and services on behalf of his organisation. In a small organisation that buying responsibility may include everything from paper clips and loo rolls to capital equipment. In a larger company it may mean he is a specialist and concentrates on buying steel and petrochemicals. The professional buyer is not a consumer of his own purchasing. The chances are that he is acting on other people's instructions and may not be technically expert about the goods he is required to purchase. Because of this the professional buyer is inclined to give the salesperson the run-around about the things which surround a purchase price, discounts, delivery, packaging, call-off arrangements and so on.

The technical buyer usually has the word 'manager' in his job title – Works Manager, Branch Manager, Office Manager. In other words, he is in the frontline and is directly accountable for his decisions, and is therefore likely to be concerned about suitability, durability, product specifications, likely sales profiles and so on. So in the main this buyer's objections will be centred on the product or

2 Difficult customers

Understand the organisation

Sometimes a customer is hesitant because he or she is not the buyer. She is there to protect the real buyer from seeing salespeople. It's important to find this out whilst keeping the apparent buyer on your side (she will probably be the buyer one day). How to find out? Read the signs – unwillingness to be specific; postponement of decision; obvious junior status. Then discreetly probe – is this procedure company policy, or is it a screen to filter out time-wasting salespeople, or to shield a misanthropic buyer? Then you can act.

Equally, make sure you know how the hierarchy works. The bigger the purchase, the more bosses may need to approve it. It may take a company weeks from the buyer accepting your proposition to the board approving the expenditure. If you know these stages, then you will know where your sale has got to, and be able to answer your own management informatively.

So you think you can sell?

Eyes and ears: innocent espionage

As you sit in Reception awaiting your customer's convenience, you can learn a lot about what's going on. Switchboard ladies and receptionists are always well (though not always accurately) informed, and usually have time for a chat. They appreciate being treated as people too, and they can tell you things that may be useful. Your fellow salesmen too, possibly rivals if it's an either/or buying pattern – always competitors, can help you both by trading information and by responding to your questions. You may find old Miss X hard to get on with until someone casually mentions he gets on much better with her since he found she was a keen bird-watcher. Reach for your Field Guide. . . . Your fellow salespeople can often give you useful information on customers' buying patterns, credit-worthiness, etc.

service and how it will meet his needs.

It's worth sparing a thought about which of these moulds the buyers you visit fit. Then plan your approach accordingly. Committees are made up of professional and technical buyers. Although the professional buyer may be the meeting coordinator and be the person who initially puts you through your selling paces, often it is the technical buyer who will scupper the deal if you can't meet and answer his product objections, or who will make the deal if he's technically satisfied, despite cost objections from the 'professional' buyer.

Let's now think about the buyer's personality and approach. First, let's consider the **Desperate Ducker**. The Ducker is the classic fence-sitter who never takes a decision unless it's the only option left. This buyer would be great on the football field; he's an expert at swerving and fast footwork and making space for himself.

He's the type who will reluctantly agree to see you and then play all sorts of tricks to get rid of you. You know the type of tricks – interruptions from secretaries about emergency meetings or overseas telephone calls.

When it gets around to actual sales objections, watch out for the emergence of the smokescreen. This buyer will automatically throw one up and hope that you won't know how to penetrate it. Once you've got past the smokescreen the chances are you will hit 'risk' as the real objection.

This is the guy who needs copperbottomed guarantees, references, site tests galore, sale-or-return arrangements and so on. He will be seeking reassurance all the way down the line and will demand, as a tactic, all sorts of contract amendments and special arrangements. Why? Well, by asking for the unusual and by demonstrating his distrust in you, your products and organisation, he knows he can send you packing for

You've got Mr Hardcase of Tippleovers at 2.30 – can I try out my salmonella poisoning trick?

The Ducker plays all sorts of tricks to get rid of you.

another month or so.

The key to understanding the ducker is anxiety. He's nervous about rows. He hates confrontations. He's terrified of being told off by his boss for doing something wrong. So it's easy to mishandle him.

Ducker: Sorry?
Salesperson: Aha! Decision day! I've got the order form. It just needs your agreement, and away we go!
Let's get the show on the road then . . . here we are!

By now the Ducker, true to form, has ducked into a cupboard, quivering with fear. He hates having to make a decision on his own responsibility. He's always looking for something to hide behind. It's usually an objection.

Ducker: Not today, thank you.
Salesperson: Why not?

*So you think
you can sell?*

Penetrating the smokescreen

The skilled salesperson will have a repertoire of means of getting past false objections.

'Leaving that to one side for a moment . . .'

'Supposing that weren't a problem . . .'

'I'd like to come back to that question, but . . .'

'That's an interesting one and I think I can give you a satisfactory answer there. But is that your only worry?'

'Well of course that's one way of looking at it. But is that the only problem?'

Ducker: Your prices are too high.

Salesperson: Too high? Our prices? Mr Ducker, I defy you to tell me where you can get custard creams for less. We've kept our macaroons on a plateau for eighteen months. At these prices our cakes will go like hot cakes. Too high? You can't be serious.

Ducker: Well, they're too high for us.

Salesperson: Oh! Too high for you! . . . Well, that's it, then. Goodbye.

No, no, no. With a ducker this might easily not be a genuine objection. You should test it to see whether it is just a smokescreen. Try side-stepping his objection – sail on past it and see whether he pulls you back. We discussed this tactic in the previous chapter when we were talking about handling objections. Let's try it out with another ducker.

Ducker: It's too expensive. It's out of the question.

Salesperson: Well, you're talking about a very sophisticated microcomputer, Mr Ducker.

Ducker: It's too expensive for us.

Salesperson: Leaving aside the question of price for the moment, is this otherwise the sort of microcomputer you're looking for?

Ducker: Well . . . er . . . I've heard . . .

Salesperson: Yes?

Ducker: No, nothing.

Salesperson: Please?

Ducker: I've heard that your back-up service isn't all it might be.

Salesperson: Ah!

See? It was a smokescreen. He was anxious about bringing up his real doubts, and giving the salesman a chance to confront them.

Let's take a look at another salesman trying to cope with a ducker . . .

Ducker: You only do it in four colours?
Oh dear!

Salesperson: Well, leaving aside the
question of colour for a moment, Mr
Ducker ... is this otherwise the kind of
robot that you're looking for?

Ducker: I'm not convinced about its
reliability. Breakdowns can be a serious
matter in a continuous high-volume
production situation like ours.

Salesperson: So if I could show you
figures proving its reliability, could we
proceed?

Ducker: Yes ... but ... when we do have
breakdowns can I be sure of your repair
and maintenance service?

Salesperson: Well, obviously you can
speak to our maintenance manager
about that but I think you'll find that
he'll guarantee you service within
twenty-four hours with penalty clauses
in the agreement if that's not the case.
So ... if you agree that our price is
competitive, and if we can satisfy you
about reliability and repair, is this the
kind of equipment that you're looking
for?

Ducker: Er ... I don't know. We've
never had it before, you see.

Salesperson: Well, of course you bloody
well haven't. I mean we'd never sell
anything to anybody if nobody bought
anything they hadn't had before. I mean
mankind would never have adopted the
wheel, would they. Oh, we don't want
to use those nasty round things. It's too
risky. We've never had it before! You
berk!

So you see, it's important not to get
personally involved. Our salesman was doing
fine until he lost control of himself. He had
uncovered all Ducker's real objections by
side-stepping, and he'd started to reassure

43

him on those. But now he's arrived at the
basic problem of anxiety – and the key to
Ducker is anxiety, right? So why not use a bit
of psychology?

Salesperson: Come on, Mr Ducker!
We're talking about a revolution in
communications. And you'll be the
leader! Up there in the forefront of
progress, blazing a trail. The intrepid
pioneer, everyone below watching you,
holding their breath! Will he do it? . . .
Can he possibly? . . . He has! Our hero!
Ducker: Not today, thank you.

Ducker doesn't want glory. He's anxious,
just terrified that he'll get it wrong. So make
his anxiety work for you. Make him anxious
about *not* buying.

Salesperson: Ah! So you've never had
one before.
Ducker: No.
Salesperson: Well, a lot of people are
going over to this kind of up-to-date
technology. I can give you the names
and phone numbers of seven customers
in this region who've installed these
robots in the past year.
Ducker: Well, I'd be prepared to suggest
to my colleagues that they might go so
far as to . . . yes I think possibly . . . I
think it's definitely maybe.
Salesperson: Ah good. Because so many
companies now are anxious . . . indeed
frightened about all this new
technology.
Ducker: Frightened of installing it?
Salesperson: No, of not installing it . . .
being left behind. It's a terrible fear.
Ducker: Is it?
Salesperson: Oh yes, I mean the job
centres are full of people who failed to
keep up with progress in this

technological age, aren't they?

Ducker: I think I might think about it.

Salesperson: Well, that would be wise, because so many companies are switching to this kind of equipment now – up-to-date, but a development of safe, sound, proven systems. Of course, I suppose . . . you could take the risk . . . of waiting for something *really revolutionary* to be developed.

Ducker: No, I don't think I want to take any risk, no, I'll think about it. In fact I think I've thought about it. I think I'll have it, I think.

You see? The salesman this time managed to exploit his anxiety and furnished him with a defence if he's called to account for his decision later.

Top Manager: Don't you think you've taken a bit of a risk, Ducker?

Ducker: This machinery is a development from safe, sound, proven models. Many of our competitors are using it, and I think there'd be a greater risk of being left behind if we didn't keep up with the times.

Top Manager: Ah yes, I see. Well done, Ducker.

So these are the rules for the Desperate Duckers:

1 Sidestep the smokescreen objections.
2 Reassure them on their genuine worries.
3 Don't fight their anxieties. Use them.

Our next customer, the **Disorganised Ditherer**, is even more difficult. He's a nice guy. Always willing to see you, even if he does keep you waiting for half an hour. Still, you persevere with booking appointments. This is the unprepared buyer. If ony he got around to collecting the facts he'd make a decision.

This is the branch manager of a shop who hasn't checked his shelves or counted his stock or analysed his sales turnover or got round to planning his shelf space to accommodate new lines. So of course he can't say 'yes' because he doesn't know what to say 'yes' to.

This is the buyer in an office or factory who promised during your last visit to attend a demonstration – but cancelled twice. Or he promised to consult a colleague about some product modifications but hasn't got around to it yet. He's the buyer who believes that a number of departments are interested in your ideas and products or services and, of course, he meant to have a meeting with them.

Ditherer: Hello. I'll be frank with you. I don't know. I can't make up my mind. I mean, I can't say that your presses would meet our very specialised printing requirements.

Salesperson: But I'm from the office cleaning firm.

Ditherer: Oh, good. Got you. Hello. Office cleaning. You called before, didn't you?

Salesperson: Last month.

Ditherer: Right. What did you tell me exactly?

Salesperson: I told you about our wide range of services and I quoted for basic cleaning on a daily, weekly or monthly basis and for more comprehensive services like upholstery cleaning, carpet cleaning . . .

Ditherer: Well, why don't you just send me some of your bumf and I'll study it.

Salesperson: I left my sales literature last month.

Ditherer: Did you? Ah, good.

Salesperson: You said you'd study it before I called this month.

Ditherer: And I will. Tell you what. Why don't you leave me some more bumf, I'll study it and then you can call again next month.

Salesperson: But I don't have any sales literature with me this time. I've already given it to you.

Ditherer: Well, give me the facts and figures, then.

Salesperson: I don't have them. I gave them to you last time.

Ditherer: So what do you carry in your briefcase, then?

Salesperson: The order form. And my lunch. Ham sandwiches.

Ditherer: What would you charge per hundred for those?

Salesperson: We aren't caterers. We're office cleaners.

Ditherer: Oh, of course, it's the other cleaners who have the catering subsidiary. They left me some bumf too, I think.

With the Disorganised Ditherer you have to be a nursemaid. Do all his thinking for him, and assume that he'll have forgotten everything you told him and lost everything you gave him:

Salesperson: Have you had a chance to study the figures that I gave you last month?

Ditherer: Well, actually, I seem to have . . .

Salesperson: Never mind. Here's another copy. Now those are the benefits in hospital and home care that your staff would be entitled to, assuming that you take the London Teaching Hospital scale.

Ditherer: Good. Yes. But I particularly asked you to produce . . . what was it?

Salesperson: The exact premiums that

your company would be paying for that kind of cover. Here they are. So do you think we can proceed on this basis?

Ditherer: Well . . . I met this chap who runs a small timber business. He was most unhappy with your scheme.

Salesperson: What was he unhappy about?

Ditherer: Something to do with illness involving long-term treatment or something like that. He said it wasn't eligible and then there were one or two people who said that your claims-handling wasn't up to scratch.

Salesperson: I see. Well look, what I suggest is this. If you'll give me a list of every single complaint and criticism that you've heard, then I will send you a very detailed case history of every instance with full explanations and justifications plus a statistical survey of our company's up-to-scratchness *vis-à-vis* the national average up-to-scratchness of our competitor companies signed by a commissioner of oaths or two justices of the peace.

NO! Our salesman is being distracted by the Ditherer's smokescreens. He can't possibly answer every hearsay objection. He should have listened to the objections and then restated them as a positive requirement.

Ditherer: I don't think this is the kind of switchboard we're looking for.

Salesperson: In what particular way doesn't it meet your needs?

Ditherer: Frankly . . . I have heard people say your stuff's unreliable. I've heard people say that old Helliwell installed one and all he had was months of crossed lines and foreign customers being cut off, very embarrassing.

Sure, it's not exactly state-of-the-art.
On the other hand, you don't need kids to set it for you . . .

Restate the Ditherer's objections positively.

Ignore the mass of tiny criticisms. Restate his objections positively.

Salesperson: So what you're looking for is a switchboard that'll prove reliable and won't need changing for many years.

Ditherer: Well, yes.

Salesperson: That's exactly what we believe this model would do. You see, it's strongly built, and it's also expandable and highly flexible – as your business grows, or changes, it'll still suit your needs. So, apart from what you may have heard from people, what specific reasons do you have for feeling that this equipment won't meet your needs?

Ditherer: Well, it's different . . .

49

Test objections

Buyers are human too. They
behave differently to strangers than
to acquaintances. They are
sometimes shy. Because you are
Mr ABC Computers or Miss XYZ
Mudshifters, they may be reluctant
to come out with criticisms – the
old British habit of saying 'sorry'
when someone steps on your toe.
Bring them to the point.

It's your job to find out what
their true aims or objections are.
Ask structured questions that
require an informative answer on
which you can build. It's not
difficult. And it enables you to
control the discussion.

Salesperson: Ah! The risk! But have you
thought of the risk of not changing?
The job centres are chock-a-block with
the most tragic cases . . .
Ditherer: Risk isn't everything. Risk
doesn't worry me.
Salesperson: What?
Ditherer: Risk doesn't worry me.
Salesperson: Well, that's torn it.

It's Mr Ducker who's frightened of risk. So
what's Mr Ditherer frightened of?

Salesperson: So what specific reason do
you have for feeling that this model
won't meet your needs?
Ditherer: Well, it's so different. We'd
have to recable the entire building and
install new phones, teach the staff how
to use them . . . You see, it would mean
that we'd have to reorganise the whole
system.
Salesperson: Yes. A lot of work.
Ditherer: Exactly. An awful lot of very
hard work.

Mr Ditherer is frightened of effort. He's
lazy. So use his laziness.

Salesperson: No sweat! We will study
your office layout and your
departmental groupings and your
available space. We'll plan it all for you
and install the switchboard and
extensions and do your staff training
and issue them with an information
booklet. So there'll be an absolute
minimum of disruption.
Ditherer: But there'll still be some
disruption.
Salesperson: Yes, but less in the long run
than if you keep this switchboard with
all its limitations.
Ditherer: So you want me to draft a letter

asking you to undertake a study such as you've proposed . . .

Salesperson: Well, actually, I've taken the liberty of preparing an order form for you. All you have to do is okay it.

Ditherer: I see, well that seems the sort of thing.

Salesperson: Your pen looks a bit heavy. Do you need a hand?

Exactly. What the Ditherer's frightened of is effort. And you can use his desire to avoid any mental effort to increase your opportunity.

So that's how to deal with Disorganised Ditherers:

1 Be a nursemaid – do as much as you can for them.
2 Restate their mass of negative criticisms positively.
3 Don't fight their laziness – use it.

Now for the third and last of our difficult customers – the **Domineering Dictator**. This one is the overbearing autocrat who likes to see salespeople squirm as he delivers another verbal barrage. He is in the know-all category, or at least that's his view of himself. This buyer enjoys taking control of the interview, lecturing the salesperson and then provoking him.

This is the man who makes wild generalisations about your company, its product or service, usually early in the interview. It's a trap. He wants to draw you into an argument before you've got anywhere near what his requirements are. He's inclined to fire questions such as: 'How much do you charge for X anyway?' early in the interview. Again, it's a trap. Answer at your peril, because he'll always say your price is too high.

Another way this buyer has of making you his victim is as follows: he likes to sound off about his knowledge of the market, but the

chances are he is not that knowledgeable –
loudmouths usually aren't. He says something you know to be incorrect – you point
this out, and however nicely you do it you'll
live to regret it. No, pointing out the error of
his ways, interrupting to display your su-
perior knowledge or answering one of his
trap questions will get you nowhere.

A skilful, low-key approach with carefully
aimed open questions is the key. Get him
talking, but on set lines, and don't lose
control. Mild flattery, if you have the
stomach for it, will go a long way and
apparent subservience even further. In this
way the Domineering Dictator will gradually
lose his guard and become more amenable.
During the time he's been stating his views
he'll also have told you a lot about his buying
philosophy, his company and their needs. So
you are in a position to propose a deal and to
think through likely objections.

Apart from all that, what are the typical
objections this type of buyer raises? Well, he
likes facts. If you don't have them or seem to
contradict yourself during the presentation
he'll be down on you like a hawk. Because he
thinks he knows it all he's likely to believe his
current suppliers are the best around – so
he'll wave the satisfaction banner. If he's
buying from you for the first time he'll be
keen to make sure that your company is
reputable. He'll have strong views on other
companies so make sure that any testimo-
nials you quote are from organisations of
which he would approve.

Let's take a look at an unfortunate
salesman who has got to deal with Mrs
Dictator.

Mrs Dictator: Enter. Sit down. Now your
despatch department's been letting us
down on delivery dates, your prices
seem to be going way over the top and
our customers tell us your products

stink. What have you got to say for
yourself? Speak up!

Salesperson: Well . . .

Mrs Dictator: What are you trying to fob
me off with this time, then?

Salesperson: Well, it's really about this
marvellous new bulldog clip. A bulldog
clip with a pedigree. Sorry. Joke.

Mrs Dictator: A joke clip, is it?

Salesperson: Oh no, no. It has a
high-tension spring which gives it a
better grip and a longer life.

Mrs Dictator: This is a very dear little
clip, isn't it?

Salesperson: Oh, you like it?

Mrs Dictator: No. I said it was dear.
Pricey.

Salesperson: But it isn't, really. It's really
reasonable.

Mrs Dictator: It's exorbitant.

Salesperson: It's reasonably reasonable.

Mrs Dictator: It's extortionate, as in
unaffordable.

Salesperson: I think it's quite cheap.

Contradiction will get you nowhere. Dictators all hold strong opinions which you're not
going to change – and you can't do much
until you find out what they are. So
encourage them to talk – they like pontifi-
cating.

Dictator: And what bric-à-brac are you
toting today? What piffling debris are
you plotting to offload on me this time?

Salesperson: Ah ha. And why should you
think, Mr Dictator, that I'd try to sell
you—

Dictator: Rubbish? Because I'm fed up
with customers coming back here
whining about the rubbish they've
bought. Because the world's gone mad
and no buck can be fast enough.

Now don't give up. Encourage him to talk. That way you'll find out about his values and his areas of pride and prejudice.

Salesperson: Well, that's very true, Mr Dictator. There's certainly a lot of rubbish about these days, I'm afraid. No doubt about that.

Dictator: You see, it's all packaging these days, all fancy display and images. Veneer, façade, camouflage. Now I'm a straightforward man, a blunt man. I believe in calling a spade a spade.

Salesperson: Funny you mention spade because . . .

Don't interrupt. Let him have his say! Once he's revealed his prejudices, you can move on to stage two: associate your product with the qualities he admires.

Salesperson: I couldn't agree with you more. As a matter of fact we pride ourselves on putting our money into performance rather than appearance. I mean, take this pair of shears, they're a bit like you in a way.

Dictator: What?

Salesperson: Straightforward. Strong. Honest. Reliable. Blunt. Well, no, not blunt. In fact sharp, extremely sharp.

And associate your opponents with the qualities he despises.

Salesperson: Of course, if you want fancy-looking implements, pretty, brightly painted stuff that looks like children's toys . . . well, there's plenty of that on the market – fancy goods at fancy prices.

Dictator: Well, I suppose they're not as bad as some of your competitors' . . .

Salesperson: Shall I put you down for a dozen?

Admitedly, Holroyd's modular
shelving systems may be a bit shaky –
but they are rather pretty.

Associate your opponents with the qualities the customer despises.

Dictator: I'll think about it.
Salesperson: What?

Even though the Domineering Dictators know what they want, you must bear in mind that there is one area in which they are not totally straightforward. They often don't want to admit that they do not have the final buying authority. So it's important to be subtle and protect their vanity.

Salesperson: So you'll think about it?
Dictator: Yes.
Salesperson: Perhaps you'll want to bring one or two colleagues in on the decision?
Dictator: Well, it's a wise person who consults his colleagues.
Salesperson: Indeed.

Are you a difficult salesperson?

This book is written from the salesperson's point of view, but spare a thought for the customer, even Mr Ducker. Remember – he has another salesperson waiting at Reception. You have only him that afternoon. What kind of salesperson are *you*? Could it be that Duckers, Ditherers, and Dictators have their equivalents on the sales side? It wouldn't make you a bad salesperson if you had similar qualities so long as you know them and use your strengths not your weaknesses. Work on your problems. If you are a Ducker, make sure you have worked out the calculations in advance – or have a cast-iron excuse for calling the office before confirmation: 'It's the end of the product run and I just have to make sure that the new batch will be at the same price.' If you are a Dictator, ensure your technique includes an element of self-mockery to take the arrogance out whilst retaining the assurance.

You can even use his vanity to your advantage. Suppose that last time he let fly about not wasting his time with fancy goods because his customers are down-to-earth people who have better things to do with their money than buy your expensive, arty-crafty items. This time, you can use that conversation to pre-empt him. Just watch his vanity . . .

Salesperson: I know there's no point in discussing the more expensive end of our range, Mr Dictator. Your clientèle wouldn't be right for that kind of merchandise, as it's rather up-market.

Dictator: I wouldn't go that far. Our clients do have taste, you know.

Salesperson: Oh. Well what shall we say, then? Half a box?

Dictator: I'll take six, at the full discount.

Salesperson: You drive a hard bargain, Mr Dictator. If our other customers were like you, we'd be out of business in three months.

So that's how you deal with Domineering Dictators:

1 Get them to reveal their prejudices.
2 Relate your products to their needs.
3 Don't fight their vanity – use it.

The difficult customers – including the Duckers, Ditherers and Dictators – may not always say yes, but at least you will have given yourself the best possible chance if you think about which category they fit into before you visit them.

Watch for the smokescreen.

Find the customer's true objections.

Use his weakness positively.

If necessary, do his thinking for him.

Keep control by asking open questions.

Adapt yourself to your customer.

Golden rules

3 'When I'm calling you' – telephone customer relations

Calling the office

It may not seem your business, but the keen salesperson who also wants to rise in the company will take an interest in its telephone answering. Ring your own company. How long before the answer? What do they say? Do you feel like a welcome customer or a nuisance? Why tolerate this when you are putting your all into effective selling?

Similarly, the best of switchboards cannot get through to an empty office. Is your sales office continuously manned? 'They're all at lunch,' is an infuriating response to a busy customer who has picked his only quiet time to ring up. Don't let your office do this to you.

So far we have looked in detail at the person-to-person sales interview. But we have not thought about selling over the telephone, which is, of course, how a great deal of modern business is done.

Although everyone knows how to use a telephone, not everyone knows how to use one properly. Judging by their telephone manner some companies think of any customer who rings them up as an enemy whose sinister intention is to do business with them. An enemy who must be thwarted at all costs! The customer is persistent and cunning, but by using the telephone he can be defeated. If you use it effectively, he'll never get through to place his order at all. So here are the rules for driving customers away.

● The first rule is not to answer the phone too quickly.
● Secondly, when you do answer, say something unintelligible . . .

Switchboard operator: 'Vers'l Nashn'l.
Bentley: Hello?
Switchboard operator: Who's calling?
Bentley: Is that Universal International?
Switchboard operator: Yes. Who do you want to speak to?
Bentley: Well, I don't really know . . .
Switchboard operator: Then I can't help you, can I?

(She leaves Bentley hanging while she answers another incoming call and then returns to him, still speaking unintelligibly.)

'Vers'l Nashn'l. Who do you want to speak to?

● Third rule – if the customer's in doubt, let him sweat it out.
● Fourth rule – put first things first. Sort out your priorities.

What's the matter with you?
Can't you hear I'm eating my lunch?!

(Bentley's phone has gone dead. He sits there, stunned, and then dials again. The phone rings for some time and finally the switchboard operator answers.)

Bentley: Hello. I'm interested in fencing.
Switchboard operator: Are you?
Bentley: Yes. Can you give me some
  information about your best quality
  overlap fencing?
Switchboard operator: Just a minute.

● Fifth rule – set him difficult questions,
  and only listen to half of the answer.

Switchboard operator: Are you
  industrial, commercial, trade, retail or
  general?
Bentley: Look, I want the department
  that does fencing. Not the woven type,
  the overlapping planks you nail to

59

cross-pieces. And I want to know how soon you can deliver.

Switchboard operator: Delivery? I'll give you Dispatch.

Bentley: No, no, hello?

Switchboard operator: Ringing for you.

Bentley: Just a minute . . .

● Sixth rule – if he's holding on and you do speak to him, don't give him time to reply.

Switchboard operator: Are you holding?

Bentley: No, it's not Dispatch that I . . . are you there?

Switchboard operator: Sorry to keep you waiting.

Bentley: Hello! Hello!

● Seventh rule – take all his inquiries as personal criticisms.

Switchboard operator: Sorry to keep you waiting.

Bentley: Don't go! Can you tell me . . .

Switchboard operator: I told you, the line's busy.

Bentley: I just want to make a quick enquiry.

Switchboard operator: We can't interrupt calls, you know.

Bentley: Then can I leave a message?

Switchboard operator: We can't take messages. You ought to know that.

Bentley: Is there anything you *can* do?

Switchboard operator: Don't shout at me. I'm just doing my job.

(Bentley tries to attract switchboard operator's attention by joggling little button on phone.)

Switchboard operator: Are you *still* holding?

Bentley: Yes.
Switchboard operator: Who are you
   ringing?
Bentley: Well, you were putting me
   through to Dispatch, but I want . . .
Switchboard operator: Dispatch? Trying
   to connect you . . .
Bentley: Oh God.
Old man: 'Spatch.
Bentley: Pardon?
Old man: 'Spatch. 'Spatch 'partment.
Bentley: I wonder if you can help me. I'm
   thinking of buying some fencing, you
   know, for a building site . . .
Old man: Well, you want Order
   Processing. 'Old on.

● Eighth rule – don't take transferring too
seriously. They can always ring back if it's
important.

*(The old man rattles the receiver, shrugs
and puts it back in the cradle.)*

Bentley: Hello, hello, operator!
Switchboard operator: Have you
   finished?
Bentley: Hello . . .

(He is cut off. Tight-lipped, he re-dials.)

Switchboard operator: 'Vers'l Nashn'l.
Bentley: Order Processing, please.
Switchboard operator: Arf a mo'. Trying
   to connect you.

*(A silly young man walks into the Order
Processing office as the phone is ringing.)*

● Ninth rule – if you can't transfer him, stall
him.

Silly young man: Hello?
Bentley: Is that the department that

takes orders for fencing?

Silly young man: Sort of.

Bentley: What do you mean 'sort of'?

Silly young man: Well, there's nobody here.

Bentley: But you're there, aren't you?

Silly young man: It's not really my department, you see. I was just in here.

Bentley: Well anyway, I want to order some fencing.

Silly young man: But I'm not really here.

Bentley: Then can you get me somebody who is really there?

Silly young man: Well, none of them seem to be here in actual fact.

Bentley: Can you at least take my name and give them a message to ring me?

Silly young man: Look, I think it would be best if you could call back when there's somebody here. Okay?

Bentley: Oh no!

(Bentley is cut off once more. Undefeated, he dials again.)

● Tenth rule – Don't let him get false ideas of his own importance.

Switchboard operator: 'Vers'l Nashn'l.

Bentley: Will you please put me through to the Managing Director?

Switchboard operator: Trying to connect you.

Secretary: Mr Gascoigne's office.

Bentley: I want to speak to Mr Gascoigne.

Secretary: Who is calling please?

Bentley: Is Mr Gascoigne there?

Secretary: Could I just have your name please?

Bentley: IS MR GASCOIGNE THERE?

Secretary: Could you just let me know what it's about?

Bentley: Is he there or is he not?

Secretary: Mr Gascoigne is a very busy man.

Bentley: So am I a busy man. A very busy man. And I want to speak to Mr Gascoigne.

Secretary: Mr Gascoigne can't speak to everybody.

Bentley: I do not want Mr Gascoigne to speak to everybody. I want him to speak to me. Is he there?

Secretary: I'll just see if he's free.

(She puts the phone down, but makes no attempt to put Bentley through to Mr Gascoigne.)

Secretary: Hello? I'm afraid there's someone with him.

Bentley: Then will you tell him I want to speak to him?

Secretary: I can't interrupt, it's someone rather important. Could you just leave your name, and I'll get him to call you back?

Bentley: My name is Bentley of Parker and Gibbs and I have been trying to . . .

Secretary: Righty-oh. We'll call you. Tarrah.

(She rings off and looks around for a pencil.)

Eleventh rule – always answer the next call before you make a note of the last one.

(The secretary starts to write 'Parker' on her pad when the phone rings again. She stops writing and answers it.)

Of course, it's just possible that you may not want to defeat the customer. You may actually welcome his approach. You may want to do business with him. In that case

63

there are only five lessons, and they're much simpler.

First lesson – answer promptly, clearly and with a smile. It's the shortest distance between two people.

Let's take a look at a different switchboard. The operator is called Jean.

Jean: Good morning. Timbertraders Limited.
Bentley: What? Who?
Jean: Timbertraders Limited.
Bentley: Oh, yes, very good.

Second lesson – find out who he needs to speak to. Remember that it may not be the person he asks for first.

Jean: Who do you want to speak to, sir?
Bentley: Speak to? Shelves. I want some shelves.
Jean: Bookshelves or factory and warehouse storage or display shelving?
Bentley: Bookshelves.
Jean: For your own use, or is it a trade enquiry?
Bentley: No, for my files and things.
Jean: May I have your name, please?
Bentley: Bentley. Parker and Gibbs.
Jean: Just one moment, Mr Bentley. I'll put you through to Mr Golledge, our sales co-ordinator.

Third lesson – don't leave him in the dark. Keep him informed, and give him a chance to reply.

Jean: His line is ringing for you now.
Bentley: Thank you.
Jean (*answering another call*): Good morning. Timbertraders Limited. No, I'm sorry, Mr Davis is at the factory. Yes, yes, any time after lunch. The

Identify the needs

Many people are crisp, clear and to the point when they ask for something. Others are not, especially if they are asking on behalf of someone else. Helpful and patient questioning will elicit what is wanted, or else the caller will realise he needs more detail from his end. In that case, offer to call him back after an agreed period.

line's still ringing, Mr Bentley.
Bentley: I see.

Fourth lesson – whatever the caller's emotions, be sympathetic. Keep your calm and keep your charm.

Jean: I'm afraid there's still no reply. Would you like to . . .
Bentley: Look. I've spent three weeks on the phone this morning. I've been misrouted, transferred, left hanging, hung up on, repulsed, frustrated and prostrated. And now you have the cheek, the gall, the effrontery . . .
Jean: I'm so sorry, Mr Bentley. I do see how inconvenient it is. Would you like to call back later, or shall I put you through to Mr Hughes of Order Processing?

So the **fifth lesson** is – give the caller a choice of the next step.

Bentley: Better put me through to Mr Hughes.

That's the way to make new customers and keep the old ones. The heart of it is that once you answer a call, you have to *make* time to deal with it effectively.

But if you are determined to foil your customers, let's look at what the expert sales-stopper can do when a customer, against all the odds, actually gets through to the person he wants.

Golledge: Hello.
Bentley: Is that the general sales office?
Golledge: Yes, Golledge speaking.
Bentley: This is Bentley, from Parker and Gibbs. Can you give me some facts and figures?
Golledge: What about?

Are you in?

The more you are seen as a help and support by your regular customers, the more likely you are to be called after hours because the stock has run out unexpectedly soon, or the machine has broken down. What do you do? Your long-suffering family want to see you; they also want to use the phone themselves. If you have many evening calls, it would be worth getting your firm to provide you with an answering machine.

Bentley: Your shelves.

Golledge: Which ones?

Bentley: I must have told half your company by now.

Golledge: Well, they didn't tell me.

Bentley: I'm considering buying some Swedish shelving, you know, the ones with reinforced aluminium. Do you possibly think you could give me some information about them?

Golledge: What sort of information?

Bentley: I don't know – facts and figures?

Golledge: We've got all the range we advertised.

Bentley: What about the brackets, you know, the shiny steel ones in your advertisement?

Golledge: Yes, we've got them.

Bentley: How much is a unit of five, six by two's, complete?

(*Golledge bangs the phone down on his desk.*)

Golledge: Where is the wretched stuff?

Secretary: What are you looking for, Martin?

Golledge: The info on that Swedish shelving for some tinpot little company.

Secretary: I filed it under 'S'.

Golledge: Right, thanks. (*To phone*) I've got the stuff here. Now, what was it you wanted to know?

Bentley: I just told you.

Golledge: Did you?

Bentley: How much is a unit of five, six by two's, complete?

Golledge: Wait a tick.

Golledge: Here it is – er – D816 . . . seventeen pounds . . .

Bentley: What??

Golledge (*to secretary*): I think this bloke's deaf or something. Seventeen pounds forty per shelf. Are you still there? Do you want some . . .

Bentley: I do not want single shelves. I want the unit of five.

Golledge: We've run out of those.

Bentley: Isn't seventeen pounds per shelf rather expensive?

Golledge: Everything's a bit expensive nowadays, isn't it? If only you'd ordered last month . . .

Bentley: Why do they cost so much?

Golledge: They cost a lot to make, I suppose. Anyway, if you want them you just fill in one of our special forms.

Bentley: Special forms? Why? I'm not ordering radar stations, only shelving.

Golledge: That's the procedure. I'll send you one. Now then . . . who are you?

Bentley: I just told you, I'm from Parker and Gibbs.

Golledge: But what's your name? Mr Rolls or something, isn't it?

Bentley: Bentley.

Golledge: Oh, Bentley. Well when you get the form just fill it up and bung it back to us. If you still want them, that is.

Margot: Martin, have you got a minute?

Golledge: Sure. *(To phone)* Hang on. What is it, Margot?

Margot: I want you to explain this new P51 form.

Golledge: Oh yes, just a tick. *(To phone)* Er – what was the address again?

Bentley: High Street, Barchester.

Golledge: . . . Barchester. *(To Margot)* It's the same as the old one, except that accounts more than three months outstanding are entered separately.

Bentley: Hello?

Golledge *(to phone)*: Sorry – just a tick.

Margot: Separately?

Golledge *(to Margot)*: Yes. In that section down there. *(To phone)* Yes?

Bentley: Look, could you tell me what other units you stock, apart from the seventeen pounds forty . . .

Golledge: Can you hang on just a couple

of minutes . . . no, listen, given me your
number and I'll call you back . . .

Bentley: My number is Barchester
six-double-o-nine.

Golledge (*writes 6099 on the back of an
envelope*): Right. Got that, I'll call you
back. Bye.

A masterly demonstration of the sales-
stopper's craft. Terrible telephone be-
haviour and hopeless sales technique.

But the telephone is such a versatile
instrument that it can be used as an aid to
making a sale as well as sales-stopping.

Secretary: General Sales. Mr Golledge's
assistant.

Bentley: This is Bentley of Parker and
Gibbs.

Secretary: Good afternoon, Mr Bentley.
May I help?
(*She writes his name down.*)

Bentley: Look, I finally got through to Mr
Golledge this morning. He said he'd
ring me straight back and that was two
hours ago. Where is he?

Secretary: I'm afraid he's still held up in
his meeting, Mr Bentley. I'm Jane
Curtis, his assistant. Perhaps I can help
you – or at least give him a message?

Bentley: What's the point of messages if
he never rings back?

Secretary: Can you tell me what it was
about?

Bentley: Your wretched aluminium-
reinforced pine shelving. I said I wanted
a unit of five. Mr Golledge says I have
to buy five singles, and I don't want to
have to buy five singles.

Secretary: What do you want to use them
for, Mr Bentley?

Bentley: Everything. All the files, the
photocopier, the dictaphone, books,
magazines, everything really.

Secretary: May I ask what kind of shelving you've got at the moment?

Bentley: Four plain shelves.

Secretary: And how are they arranged?

Bentley: Just one on top of the other.

Secretary: Doesn't that make the bottom one rather too low – or the top one too high?

Bentley: It is a bit high for the girls – but they can always stand on a chair.

Secretary: Is there any other free wall space?

Bentley: The next wall's only got a chart on it. Why?

Secretary: I was wondering whether even five will give you enough room. As you know we don't have the units of five in stock at the moment, but wouldn't the top shelf of five be really quite difficult to get at – especially for the secretaries?

Bentley: Well, if they had to get things from the *very* top shelf . . .

Don't make your training too obvious

People like dealing with people. Up against a system, they can get nervous. Telephone sales training is excellent and desirable but don't let it turn you into a script-reader. It is easy to spot those learned-by-rote introductions and they act as a red light to buyers: 'Be on your guard. She's going to sell me something!'

At the first stroke I will put a smile in my voice and start offering you a range of alternative purchases.

Don't show your training too obviously.

Secretary: And if four shelves aren't
enough at the moment, won't you find
five are getting rather crowded before
long?

Bentley: What do you suggest?
*(She has been making notes and is now
looking through the catalogue.)*

Secretary: We have a very attractive and
very convenient corner unit of two
threes, which sounds much more like
what you want.

Bentley: But that makes six, and I only
want five.

Secretary: On the other hand, a corner
unit would give you room to expand,
and make it much easier to reach the
top shelf – even easier than now. Do
you want it on account or would you
rather pay cash?

Bentley: Hold on – what does it cost?

Secretary: With the polished aluminium
brackets and stainless steel fittings it
comes to £99.90, and we can deliver it
at the end of the week. Would you like
us to fit it, or would you rather do it
yourself?

Bentley: A hundred pounds for a set of
shelves? I'm sure there are people who
do it for less than that.

Secretary *(looking at her notes)*: You did
say you'd be keeping a photocopier on
them?

Bentley: Yes.

Secretary: Then I think you'll find the
added strength of the reinforcing plates
and double brackets is well worth the
small extra cost.

Bentley: It seems a lot to pay.

Secretary: It isn't really, when you
consider how much longer they'll last,
and the cheaper ones do start sagging
after a while. These are very strong,
and they do look smart. I'll pass your
order on to Dispatch straight away, and

you can have it this week. May I have the delivery address please, Mr Bentley?

Bentley: High Street, Barchester.

Secretary: A three-shelf corner unit for Mr Bentley, Parker and Gibbs, High Street, Barchester. Is that the invoice address as well?

Bentley: Yes.

Secretary: And may I have your telephone number?

Bentley: Barchester six-double-o-nine.

Secretary: Six-o-double-nine.

Barchester: No, six-double-o-nine.

Secretary: Sorry. Thank you. Would you like them Thursday afternoon or Friday morning?

Bentley: Thursday afternoon would be fine.

Secretary: I'll see you get them. Tell me, is there anyone else in your company who might need shelving?

Bentley: I wouldn't know. You'd have to ask Office Management.

Secretary: Who would that be?

Bentley: Peter Dyson, I suppose.

Secretary: Fine. Now, is there any other timber requirement apart from shelving that we might be able to help you with?

Bentley: Not unless you do fencing. But that's not your line, is it?

Secretary: Not in this department, but our industrial division deals with fencing. Shall I get them to call you?

Bentley: *Them* call *me.* Oh, yes, please.

Secretary: It'll be Mr Foster or Mr McRae, and I'll be on to them as soon as I've told Dispatch about your shelving. Now, is there anything else I can help you with?

Bentley: No thank you – that's marvellous. *Them* call *me* . . .

Secretary: Thank you, Mr Bentley. Goodbye.

So that's the telephone. A sales-stopper or a sales-maker – whichever you want.

Golledge: Anyone call while I was out?
Secretary: Mr Bentley.
Golledge: I said I'd ring him, didn't I?
Secretary: That's okay, I sold him a corner unit of two threes.
Golledge: Six shelves! He said he only wanted five. They pick up the phone and expect you to read their minds ...

I'd like to place a small ad:
'Would the gentleman from
  • Birmingham who
   • ordered 5000
    • metering valves
       from Stonewick Ltd
       please phone Lizzie
       on 01 637 06 ...

Check back the details.

When answering the telephone:

Answer promptly, clearly and politely.

Find out who the caller needs to speak to and ask his name and company, when it's appropriate.

Don't leave him in the dark – tell him what you're going to do and give him a chance to speak.

Be sympathetic and keep calm.

If you can't put him through to the right person, give him the choice of what is to be done next.

When the customer has been put through to you:

Explore the customer's needs, asking open questions.

If you haven't got what he asks for, offer the nearest alternatives that you do have.

Have the information to hand – always.

Stress the benefits of the product.

Meet price objections with value answers.

Check back all the important details.

And before you ring off explore other sales possibilities – other customers for the product, and other products for the customer.

Golden rules

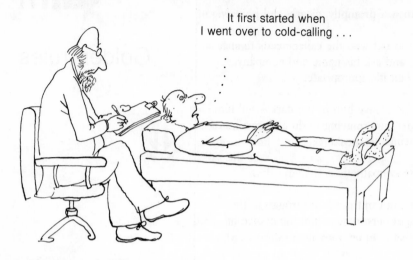

It first started when
I went over to cold-calling . . .

Many people find cold-calling more unnerving than any other type of selling.

Many salespeople find cold-calling more unnerving than any other type of selling. Ringing up people you don't know, trying to persuade them to buy something that they may not think they want is obviously an uninviting prospect. But it is a necessary part of many selling operations, and mastering the cold call has led to swift promotion for many people.

To find out the sort of mistakes that cold-callers can make, and how to avoid these pitfalls, let's take a look at the sales office of Parker and Gibbs. There are two salesmen in the office this Monday morning – Arnold Moss, a bright young man who has been cold-calling for several months, and Martin Mathews, an older salesman who has had to be taken off the road as part of the company's cut-backs.

Miss A: Good morning, Mr Moss. Ah, Mr Mathews, isn't it?

Mathews: It is indeed. What can I do for you?

Miss A: I've got a memo for you both, from the Sales Director. We've got a warehouse full of the small stainless steel fastenings and he wants you to push them as hard as you can. There's your stock list and your Yellow Pages.

Matthews: Cor!

Miss A: Anything wrong?

Mathews: Nothing, nothing.

Miss A: I'm sure Mr Moss will give you any help you need.

Mathews: You lift this bit up and speak into there, don't you? Marvellous. Yellow Pages? Huh. I'll call old Fisher, Works Manager at U.I. I happen to know he needs some of this stuff.

Moss: I wish I had your contacts. I'll have to start from square one.

Mathews: Years of experience do count, you know. Hello, is that Universal

4 The cold call – telephone sales

Motivation

Your job is often solitary. Up and off in the morning with a lot of prospective or established customers. Your manager is in his office worrying if you are motivated enough. How can you motivate yourself?

Have objectives: for the customers (I'll sell Bloggs 20 cases of butter); for the day (I'll sell 200 cases of butter today). These targets help your sales, keep you on your toes, and make the day more fun.

Vary your routine: Perhaps you use one day in five for 'cold-calling'. Try instead to fit in one 'cold call' a day, for a week. Don't get in a rut.

On the doorstep

Would Martin Matthews do any
better on the doorstep – 'See 'em
to sell 'em,' in his own words? Not
too likely. Unless the business is
very small, there will be a
receptionist who asks the dreaded
question, 'Have you an
appointment?' Show her that
you're something special. 'We're
carrying out a survey of industry
needs in this area. I'm sorry I
couldn't make an appointment, but
it will really take up very little of his
time.' If he's in a meeting, use the
'I'm not in Barchester very long,
but could come back at four-thirty'
technique.

The more the receptionist feels
that you are a serious caller whom
her manager might be interested
or even glad to talk to, the more
likely you are to get through. See if
you can get a word on the internal
telephone. If all else fails, leave
your information, and card, in a
sealed envelope with his name on
it, and telephone back to check
that he's had it and read it; and
make an appointment.

International? I want to speak to Mr
Fisher.

1st woman: I'll put you through to his
assistant.

Mathews: No, don't! Oh God!

. . .

Moss: Good morning, this is Arnold
Moss from Parker and Gibbs. I wonder
whether you can give me some
information.

. . .

Mathews: They've put me through to
Fisher's assistant. I didn't want to talk
to him, it's that idiot Freddie . . . Oh,
hello Freddie – I was just talking about
that idiot Freddie . . . oh, what's his
name . . .

Freddie: Who are you, what do you want?

Mathews: Nothing. I just want to speak
to Mr Fisher.

Freddie: He's not available.

Mathews: Where is he?

Freddie: Who is this?

Mathews: Er – forget it. I'll call back.
Silly idiot. (*He hangs up.*) You see, it's a
complete waste of time. You've got to
see 'em to sell 'em.

Moss: I'll call him on Monday at ten
then. Thank you so much. Goodbye.
Sorry, I didn't hear you. I was on the
phone. How did you get on?

Mathews: I didn't get through to him. I'd
have sold him if I had. It's a waste of
bloody time, fishing names out of the
phone book. What's the use if you don't
know who to speak to. (*He dials a
number.*)

2nd woman: Good morning, Coggan
International.

Mathews: Er, hello, this is Parker and

Gibbs, we make and supply industrial fastenings. Can I interest you?

2nd woman: No thank you. Goodbye.

Matthews: Wonderful, isn't it? You could do that all day.

Moss: I usually find it helps to ask to be put through to the man responsible for the buying.

Mathews: Don't you worry about me. (*He dials again.*)

3rd woman: Hello, Robinson Automation.

Mathews: Good morning. I wonder if you can help me.

3rd woman: With pleasure.

Mathews: Would you please put me through to the man responsible for buying.

3rd woman: Hold on, please.

Girl: Mr Stutter's secretary.

Mathews: Who's he? Is he the chap responsible for buying?

Vending machines?
No thanks.

It helps to be put through to the buyer.

Girl: Yes.

Mathews: What did you say his name was?

Girl: Arthur Stutter. But he's rather tied
up at the moment. May I help you?

Mathews: Well, we manufacture and
supply industrial fastenings.

Girl: Are you a salesman?

Mathews: Er . . .

Girl: Mr Stutter is unavailable all day.
Would you mind writing in?

Mathews: I'd rather speak . . .

Girl: Thank you for calling. Good
morning.

Mathews has completely failed to consider
the special techniques necessary for
successful cold-calling. It is not just
ordinary selling, and an extra handicap is
that you can't see the customer. When you
are cold-calling, even getting through to
the right buyer is often a battle.

Moss: And who is responsible for buying
your manufacturing components?

4th woman: Mr Bishop.

Moss (*making a note*): Mr Bishop. Thank
you. Would you put me through to him,
please . . .

Bishop's secretary: Mr Bishop's office.

Moss: Good morning. This is Arnold
Moss, from Parker and Gibbs. May I
speak to Mr Bishop?

Bishop's secretary: What is it about,
please?

Moss: Oh, isn't he there? Could you tell
me what time he'll be back, please?

Bishop's secretary: Oh well, he's here,
but he's in a meeting. Can I help?

Moss: It's rather complicated. I need
some information from him – would it
be best if I called back this afternoon or
tomorrow morning?

Bishop's secretary: Oh well, this
afternoon should be all right.

Moss: About three o'clock?

Bishop's secretary: Fine.

Moss: Thank you. Goodbye.

Mathews: Get through to the person responsible, eh?

Moss (*making a note*): I will do, at three o'clock. His secretary is committed now to putting me through.

Mathews: I'd better try to speak to old Fisher again.

When you are cold-calling you cannot build up the sort of friendly rapport that often occurs when you are selling in person. No one wants to waste time over small talk with a stranger on the telephone.

Fisher: Fisher here.

Mathews: Hello there, Mr Fisher, I'll get straight to the point, I'm glad I've got through to you at last . . .

Fisher: Who is that?

Mathews: Didn't she say? This is Mathews.

Fisher: Mathew who?

Mathews: No, no, Martin Mathews, Parker and Gibbs. That's my firm. Well, it's not mine, not yet anyway. Still, it's a miserable day, isn't it? What's it like your end?

Fisher: Er . . .

Mathews: It's nice to be sitting in a warm office for once.

Fisher: *What-do-you-want?*

Mathews: I'll get straight to the point. Actually, I've been trying to get hold of you all day – they put me through to Freddie Onslow . . .

Fisher: Look, I've got a meeting with my chairman, I've got to go.

Mathews: But I want to speak to you. It's about our stainless steel fastenings.

Fisher: Call me back at one o'clock. OK?

79

Records

The customer record cards you keep are a vital part of your armoury. Remember 'research the customer'? On the card you should note:

- Name
- Address
- Telephone number
- Details of how to find, if complicated
- Customer's name
- Assistant's name
- Type of customer: wholesale, chain, retail etc.
- Call frequency
- Date of last call
- Early closing
- Quarterly sales figures
- Special comments

Take the day's cards with you, attaching any other relevant papers: a copy of the previous order sheet, the basic list of your products that this customer orders, etc.

Mathews: I got a commitment. He'll speak to me at one o'clock.

. . .

Moss: I wish I had your gift of the gab.
Mathews: I've been at it a few years now, you know.
Moss: I'm not much good at talking. I'm more of a listener.
Mathews: You've got to be able to chat a bit, you know, especially when you're selling bloody boring things like nuts and bolts.
Moss: But the people who need them don't think they're boring.

. . .

Mathews: Sold any yet?
Moss: Only a couple of thousand. You?
Mathews: I haven't had much luck, yet.
Moss: I once made twenty-six calls in a row without making a single sale. Do you bother to keep record cards?
Mathews: What?
Moss: You know, who you've called, and what they said.
Mathews: I haven't sold anything, so there isn't much to record, is there?
Moss: But will you remember what they said, when you call them back? Wish I could.
Mathews: I make notes sometimes. But what are we supposed to be, a two-man market research organisation?
Moss: I suppose we are. That's very clever.

In fact, Moss is cleverer than Mathews. He knows that the real battle in cold-calling is to get your customer interested. It is too easy for them to just hang up!

Moss: Good morning, Mr McKay. This is Arnold Moss from Parker and Gibbs. We supply industrial fastenings. I gather your European sales have been going up very fast in the past year?

McKay: Yes, they have. Are you trying to sell me something?

Moss: I'm in business just like you are, Mr McKay, but what I really wanted in the first instance was some information. . . . Apart from your heavy-duty rotavators, what other products have you been manufacturing?

McKay: Quite a wide range of agricultural machinery.

Moss (*making notes*): I see. And how regularly have you been receiving your supplies of fastenings?

McKay: Well, disputes and shortages allowing, we usually order two to three months in advance.

Moss: Would you mind telling me what your average monthly requirement is?

McKay: I'll find out. Hold on.

Moss: With pleasure.

Mathrews: You're being a bit nosey, aren't you?

Moss: He's interested, because he's talking about his own business. And I'm discovering whether he's interested in finding a new supplier.

Mathews: Yes, I've got the message.

. . .

Mathews: How long have you been making lawnmowers, Mr Evans?

Evans: Sixty-three years.

Mathews: And do you make other machinery?

Evans: Yes.

Mathews: And do you get your fastenings from one regular supplier?

Evans: Yes.

81

Is your company less than perfect?

Even good companies can have problems in specific areas. Computer breakdowns. Overstretched warehouse. New lines that sometimes fail to find acceptance. These can seriously affect your ability to sell. At the same time, it's basically a good oufit and you want to stay on and be promoted. Sell your way round the problem. Make the most of your benefits: product, service, established relationship. Don't dismiss the problem but emphasise what is being done to tackle it and set it in a time perspective. Never denigrate other parts of the company, whatever the provocation. Point out the cause of the problem – success and huge demand – if that helps. Point out that everyone's computer gives problems sometimes – if that helps. Above all, show yourself as reliable, concerned, loyal to your company, and doing your utmost to protect your customer: 'Orders are stacking up but if you can round yours up to 150 packs, I can get a special delivery arranged, bypassing the backlog . . .'

Mathews: Why?

Evans: Because it's convenient, that's why. And it's none of your business anyway.

Mathews: Sorry, sorry, not meaning to criticise. I was just asking because we also make industrial fastenings. Are you happy with your present supplier?

Evans: Harold Hastings? We've been having a bit of delivery trouble.

Mathews: Oh them! They're a bit hopeless sometimes, aren't they?

Evans: No, they're not hopeless at all.

Mathews: Of course not. But you might be interested in a new supplier?

Evans: I might be.

Mathews: Good, because we'd be interested in supplying you.

Evans: So we're both interested.

Mathews: Well, that's very interesting. Shall I put something in the post, then?

Evans: Sure. Is that all? 'Bye.

It is fatal to criticise the customer's present supplier. If you are rude about them they will be even more so about you. It's much better to point out the advantages of your own company. And having got the customer interested, make a date for a rep to visit them if you can't close the deal there and then.

Moss: Our factory can certainly manufacture that sort of volume. I'll send you a quotation.

McKay: It's all rather complicated. There are temperature-resistance problems. And we've got an unusual tooling set-up here.

Moss: Well, I'll tell you what, Mr McKay. I'll have one of our representatives call round and he can see your set-up and show you some examples of our special jobs.

McKay: I'm not sure it's worth his trouble . . .

Moss: It's no trouble. What about Thursday week – is the morning or the afternoon best for you?

McKay: Afternoons are better really.

Moss: Let's say Tuesday the 4th at three o'clock. It'll be Mr Marriott.

McKay: Right you are. Goodbye, then.

Moss: Goodbye, Mr McKay, and thank you very much indeed.

Mathews: I've got a Mr Evans at Becket Lawnmowers interested.

Moss: Good. Is he sending in an order, or did you book a visit?

Mathews: I . . . er . . . yes . . .

(Sighing, Mathews dials again.)

Mathews: Extension 386, please.

Evans: Evans here.

Mathews: Hello, it's me again. Look, there's a couple of things I forgot to tell you. First of all . . .

Evans: Who is that, please?

Mathews: It's me, Martin Mathews from Parker and Gibbs. We were talking just now about the possibility of our supplying your fastenings, remember now?

Evans: Yes.

Mathews: I thought you would be interested to know that nowadays we're part of a huge corporation with an annual turnover of £700 million. We've had a Queen's Award for Industry.

Evans: We're a very small company, we're not in your league.

Mathews: We supply a lot of small companies.

Evans: No, I wouldn't want to be in a queue behind Shell and ICI.

Mathews: You wouldn't be.

83

Evans: Look, boyo, I tell you what. We're
fully stocked at the moment, call back
in June. We'll talk about it then.

Mathews: But I've got a warehouse full
now.

Evans: It's the best I can do. 'Bye.

. . .

Moss: Would you do me a favour,
Martin?

Mathews: What?

Moss: These three call-backs. All these
companies have expressed interest, all
the details of my previous calls are on
these cards, and they all wanted to be
called back today.

Mathews: How do you remember that?

Moss: I noted the dates in my diary. I set
them up, but they're all first-class
prospects, so I think a salesman could
handle them.

Mathews (*his confidence returning*): OK.
Fine.

. . .

Mathews: Last month, Mr Riley, you
talked to one of my colleagues about
buying some fastenings from us. I
wonder if you've made up your mind
yet?

Riley: No, I haven't. Not yet. Cheerio.

. . .

Mathews: Good morning, Mr Wolsey.
This is Martin Mathews, Parker and
Gibbs. A couple of weeks ago you asked
us to send you some of our literature.
Have you received it yet?

Wolsey: No.

Mathews: What?

Wolsey: No, I haven't. Sorry. 'Bye.

Always, always, always ask open questions that keep the customer talking.

Mathews (*with mounting desperation*):
Good morning, Mr Pope, this is Martin Mathews of Parker and Gibbs. Last week you asked us to send you some literature and I'm *sure* you've read it by now. What did you think of it?

Pope: No, I haven't had time to read it yet.

Mathews: *Why not?* Sorry, I was, er, talking to someone in the office. So let's go over the situation. You need regular supplies of stainless steel fastenings, is that so?

Pope: Yes.

Mathews: And you've been worried about your usual suppliers, because they're always going on strike.

Pope: Right.

Mathews: So, have you considered buying from us?

Pope: Yes, but in your case I'm worried about the cost.

Mathews: Well that's no problem, I assure you. We give very significant discounts to companies buying large quantities on call-off, and secondly the units per ton are high because they are lightweight, so they work out at least as cheap as the competition and in many cases quite a lot cheaper. So if you could just give me the gauge and quantity you want, I'll have them round to you by . . .

Pope: I don't like to be rushed. If I want to order any I'll get in touch, all right? Thank you for calling.

. . .

Moss: How have you been doing?

Mathews: None of them were remotely

Are you effective?

All those miles you clock up are very expensive. And time-consuming. If you are keen to improve your sales figures, it's worth looking hard at how you spend your day. Divide it into fifteen-minute sections and plot each day for a fortnight, noting driving time, waiting time and true selling time. You may be very surprised at how little of the day you spend face-to-face with a customer. If you have to drive more than fifty miles during potential selling time, you should replan.

interested. I don't know why you
thought they were.
Moss: Oh.
Mathews: I was right all along. Selling on
the telephone is a total waste of time.

He's absolutely right, of course. It is a total
waste of time if you do it his way. Watch the
mistakes.

● First, no preparation:

Mathews: I'll call old Fisher.

● Then selling to the wrong person:

Woman: Good morning, Coggan
International.
Mathews: Er, hello, this is Parker and
Gibbs, we make and supply industrial
fastenings. Can I interest you?
Woman: No thank you.

● Wasting time with chit-chat:

Mathews: I'll get straight to the point.
Actually, I've been trying to get hold of
you all day – they put me through to
Freddie Onslow . . .

● Not making a record of information
gained:

Mathews: I haven't sold anything, so
there isn't much to record, is there?

● Asking questions with yes/no answers:

Mathews: And do you make any other
machinery?
Evans: Yes.

● Running down their existing suppliers:

Mathews: Oh them! They're a bit
hopeless sometimes, aren't they?
Evans: No, they're not hopeless by any
means.

● Failure to try and convert interest into an
order:

Evans: So we're both interested.
Mathews: Well, that's very interesting.
Shall I put something in the post, then?

● Not tailoring your information to the
person you're talking to:

Mathews: I thought you would be
interested to know that nowadays we're
part of a huge corporation with an
annual turnover of £700 million.
Evans: We're a very small company, we're
not in your league.

● Inviting rejection:

Mathews: I wonder if you've made up
your mind yet?
Riley: No, I haven't. Not yet. Cheerio.

● Rushing into sales pitch:

Mathews: So they work out at least as
cheap as the competition and in many
cases quite a lot cheaper. So if you'd
like to give me the gauge and quantity
you want . . .

It was a total waste of time. Of course, it
doesn't have to be. Let's take another look at
Moss, the master of the cold call, in action.

Moss: Oh, it's one o'clock. Isn't that
when you said you'd call your friend
Fisher back?

Territory planning

If you have a hundred customers,
spread over three counties, each
requiring a monthly call by
appointment, how do you plan to
get around? You might think you
work methodically through –
North–South or East–West. This is
better than random strikes, but
even better would be to quarter
your territory and plan to spend
two days in one quarter, and the
next two in the opposite quarter.
This gives you the chance both to
catch up on a cancelled
appointment in the first area, and
to respond to any urgent call from
elsewhere in the territory without
having to go so far out of your
way, as you cross it twice a week
anyway. Day 5 is either added to
the second two-day plan, making
three, or is used for close-to-home
customers, or for cold calls.

Territory Map

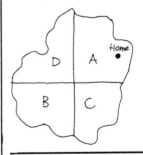

Mathews: Tough! (*He takes a mouthful of
a sandwich.*) I'm having my lunch.

Moss: May I call him, then? I think one
of us should call him back at the agreed
time.

Mathews: Be my guest.

The first rule of cold-calling is to
prepare beforehand. Do your research and
have all the information you need in front
of you. Find out the name of the buyer, if
you don't already know it, *before* you are
put through to him. And hold your fire
until you can talk to the buyer himself.
There's no point in trying to sell steel
fastenings to the telephonist! When you
finally talk to the buyer, don't blunder
straight into selling.

Moss: Good afternoon, Mr Fisher. This
is Arnold Moss from Parker and Gibbs.
My colleague Martin Mathews spoke to
you this morning and you asked him to
call you back. Unfortunately he's
unavailable at the moment so he's asked
me to take this over. He wanted to talk
to you about our stainless steel
fastenings.

Fisher: Ah. Yes.

Moss: I see from the Engineering Digest
that you've just landed a big contract in
Brazil. If you're supplying the motor
and aircraft industries you must need a
steady flow of supplies.

Fisher: That's right.

Show that you know about his company
– everyone is susceptible to flattery!

Moss: I wonder if I could ask what sort of
fastenings you have been using, mostly.

Fisher: Some mild steel. Some brass.
Some stainless steel.

Moss: What sort of sizes?

Fisher: M5 by 1mm up to M24 by 100mm, chiefly.
Moss: And how has the supply been?
Fisher: Patchy. Up and down, you know.
Moss: And what about when you start the Brazilian deliveries?
Fisher: Well, that's a good question.

Explore his past problems and future worries, and record the information you are gathering. Avoid asking yes/no questions – you want to get him to talk about the business. Try to build up a picture of his operation, so that you don't waste time offering him goods he does not want. Underline the benefits of buying from *your* company.

Moss: How important is it going to be to you to have regular punctual deliveries of guaranteed quality?
Fisher: That's the name of the game, chum.
Moss: You see, Mr Fisher, I think we may be able to help you on this. You probably know we're very large stockists of your gauge of fastening, so we have constant stocks and regular deliveries and . . .
Fisher: Steady on, I can't change suppliers just like that. We've been dealing with Harper and Smith for twenty years or more.
Moss: No, I was just thinking that with this new contract you could take us on as a second supplier. You know, keep both companies on our toes. That way, if one company has a delivery problem you've got a reserve . . . so if you'd just like to place a trial order . . .

Finally – take an order, or at least get him to commit himself to the next step.

Fisher: But I think your prices are probably too high for us.

Moss: Well, how much have you been paying per 1000 for, say, 5mm by 12mm and 18/8 stainless.

Fisher: About £100, and you charge more like £125, don't you?

Moss: If you can guarantee us a total offtake of, say, 30,000 a year, you can call them in by the thousand at £110.

Fisher: Really? That's very interesting.

Moss: Do you want the first thousand in M5 12mm or M6 25mm?

Fisher: The next order I was going to place was for 1250 M24 by 100mm bolts.

Moss (*checking list*): That's fine. We've got plenty of those in stock.

Fisher: But could you deliver them next week?

Moss: Do you want them next week?

Fisher: I do really.

Moss: Then we'll have them to you on Wednesday or Thursday. We'll invoice at the standard rate, but we'll credit you with the balance when we get the year's guarantee. Was it cheesehead or hexagon you wanted?

Fisher: Hexagon.

Moss: Fine. That's 1250 M24 by 100mm hexagon bolts in 18/8 stainless to Mr Fisher at Universal International next Wednesday or Thursday at the latest. Thank you very much, Mr Fisher.

Fisher: Thank you, Mr Moss.

So there it is – cold-calling does not have to be a waste of time.

Later on, in Parker and Gibbs' sales office . . .

Miss A: How's it going?

Mathews: Fine. We just made a big sale to U.I.

Miss A: Splendid. Both of you?

Mathews: No. It was my customer, but Arnold tied up the loose ends very capably. I did the original chatting-up, of course.

Miss A: I see. Mr Moss, the Sales Director wants to see you right away.

Moss: Oh dear.

Mathews: Hope you're not getting the push, old boy.

Miss A: No, he's getting a bonus.

Mathews: A bonus? Him? He never sold anyone anything.

Miss A: No, but people do seem to buy things from him, don't they?

The home office

Lucky the salesperson who has his own study/office. Most of us fight with the rest of the family for a corner of the living-room table. And yet it's the basis of your effectiveness. Keep it simple and clear. Customer cards. Order files. Queries awaiting answers. Current samples and literature. Expenses record. Stationery. Blank order forms. Envelopes. It doesn't matter if you keep it in a filing cabinet or in a suitcase under the bed. If it's a mess you won't want to look at it. And your results will suffer.

If your filing cabinet is a mess, you won't want to look at it.

Golden rules

Prepare for a call by doing your research. Make sure that you have all you may need within reach.

Find out the name of the buyer before asking to be connected.

Hold your fire till you talk to the buyer.

Give some brief information about your company, and show that you know something about them.

Collect and record information with questions in the past tense, and avoid yes/no questions.

Explore past problems and future worries.

Underline benefits.

Finish by taking an order or getting a commitment to the next step.

If the product you are selling does something – whether it is a tin-opener or a computer – you will probably have to demonstrate its use. Your customer will naturally want to see for himself what it can do. This should be perfectly straightforward, but it is surprising how many sales demonstrations are badly handled. And a good demonstration can do more to persuade a customer to buy than any amount of salesman's blarney. So in this chapter we are going to consider how you should – and shouldn't – run a sales demonstration.

5 The show business

Hang on – maybe this one works!

It's surprising how many sales demonstrations are badly handled.

Let's look, first of all, at a photocopier showroom, where a potential customer has an appointment for a demonstration.

Customer: I think you're expecting me.
Fred: Am I?

*So you think
you can sell?*

Visual aids

The machine or product itself is the ultimate visual aid. Sometimes it's too big to transport, or too expensive. Sometimes it's not ready at the time you're selling it. So you need to display its capacities without exhibiting it. Did you know that most people take in about 11 per cent of what they hear, and retain 20 per cent of that? But that the retention factor of what they read or see is more like 80 per cent? That's why it's worth carrying literature and pictures in your bag (and always having duplicate sets for the Ditherers who lose them).

Even in the showroom the customer will probably want to take some convincing and attractive information away – he probably has a boss or committee to convince.

The sales force does not produce the hand-outs. But if they're not what you need, you should make it known. Suffer in silence, and you'll get the blame if your company's literature is no good.

Customer: My secretary rang to fix a demonstration of your 2300 copier.

Fred: A demonstration? We can do those any time, no need to book anything special. The 4600?

Customer: No, the 2300.

Fred: That one? All right.

Customer: I'm with Universal International Management Services Department. What I'm really interested in . . .

Fred: Good, well, the 2300 is just over here. First-rate machine, very popular. Clear, quick and simple to operate. Any fool can work one, it's very simple. You just . . . Marjorie! could you ask Charlie to come along? Won't be a moment . . . marvellous chap, Charlie, he can fix anything. Well, the 2300 is a fully automated electrostatic copier – ah, Charlie. We're having a little trouble starting up the old 2300 . . .

Charlie: Well, this is only a display model – it's a customer reject. Not meant to work . . .

Fred: Well, this customer wants a demonstration, so . . .

Charlie: Why didn't someone tell me they wanted it tarted up for demo jobs? Display only, that's what they said . . .

(Charlie fiddles about with the machine and leaves, grumbling to himself.)

Fred: Where were we? Oh yes. The 2300 is an electrostatic copier operating with a conventional oxide-coated paper, but fed internally . . .

Customer: Could I see it copy something?

Fred: Good idea. Copy something. Right, off we go, the 2300 is an electrostatic copier operating with a conventional . . .

Customer: But actually, er . . .

Fred: It's fed from a magazine within the

machine. It accepts biro, pen, pencil, felt-tip, typed matter, coloured illustrations, solids and half-tones and produces the requisite number of crisp black and white copies.

Customer: But it's pink.

Fred: Pink?

Customer: And it's got holes.

Fred: I should have said. Offset litho masters can be produced if required.

Customer: But I just need a straightforward copier.

Fred: Oh I see. Well, you've just got to use this paper instead of that . . .

Customer: Can I work it myself?

Fred: If you want to, but *you* won't be using it, will you? It'll be the secretary girls, won't it? You just press that . . . and a full range of colours and densities are reproduced swiftly and clearly on the standard A4 international paper size sheet or from a continuous feed stack in the A4 width.

Customer: What did you say it costs?

Fred: Er, there's a revised price list somewhere.

Customer: It's the price per copy that really interests me.

Fred: It's very competitive. First-class value. And its tremendously tough . . . mustn't waste electricity. Actually, this one is a bit . . . you know . . . but they're very tough. Like a look at the works? Well, that's the 2300.

Customer: I wonder what would happen if we . . .

Fred: Pretty self-explanatory, really, isn't it? Any other model I can show you?

Customer: No, it was just the 2300 I wanted to see.

Fred: Good, well, there it is.

Customer: Yes . . .

Fred: So that's it, then. Very nice to meet you.

How does your showroom look?

Awful, if Fred's in charge. But you're the salesperson who uses it too. Do you say, 'This lot can't even set up a showroom,' or do you say, 'I can't sell properly in this sort of environment, and I want it changed'? Remember that Rolls Royce? It was never attained by someone who said, 'It's no good *me* complaining: they'll never listen.' Make sure that the company's showroom reflects the company's view of its products.

That's one way of demonstrating. The Fred
way. Fred made most of the mistakes that
drive any audience away. But the biggest
mistake of all was the first one – the starting
point of any demonstration. He never asked
the question, 'Why?' Why does the customer
want to see the demonstration? Why has he
come to see your show? You can't even
rehearse your performance until you know
why he's interested.

Let's take a simple example – a water stall.

Fred: Good morning sir, madam.
Customer: I'm very interested in this
water stuff of yours.
Fred: It's absolutely marvellous. Let me
show you . . . You see, you can cook
food with it . . . like this . . . you can put
it on plants to make them grow, and
you can clean stains off shiny surfaces
with it or you can mix it with any of
these and make pictures with it . . . or,
look, you can brush your teeth or wash
your hands with it . . . you can even
keep goldfish in it . . . isn't it
marvellous?
Customer: Yes . . . thank you very much.
Madam: It's very good, isn't it, dear?
Customer: But I actually wanted
something to drink.
Fred: You see, ladies and gentlemen, you
can cook food in it . . .

No matter how simple the product is, you
don't know what to show the customer, what
points to make, until you know why he's
interested.

Now let's move on to the garden department of a big store.

Basil: These are all electric of course, sir.
Customer: You just press the button?
Basil: That's right. Do you have a mower
at the moment, sir?

Customer: Yes, I do.

Basil: May I ask why you're thinking of getting another?

Customer: Well, it's clapped out.

Basil: Have you had it long?

Customer: About three years.

Basil: I see. And do you have a big lawn?

Customer: The garden's mostly grass, and it takes a devil of a time to do.

Basil: And you prefer an electric mower, do you?

Customer: Yes, I don't want one of those petrol things.

Basil: If I could show you a mower that could save you about a third of your time and last rather longer than three years, would it be of interest to you?

Customer: Well . . .

Basil: Firstly, you can see that this model is a third wider than the other . . . that means you can cut your lawn in fewer passes, and so it takes that much less time. Secondly . . .

Basil is floundering – he doesn't know what to demonstrate because he doesn't know which aspect of the product might interest the customer.

Every stage of the demonstration must have a specific point to prove, otherwise it's useless.

Now let's think about the technique of the demonstration itself. It's not hard to pick up if you think of the demonstration as a three-act play. The three acts are quite simple:

1 Before.
2 During.
3 After.

So let's start with Act One – **Before** . . . and that just means preparation. Remember Fred?

Who receives the customers?

If it's you – fine. If it's the receptionist – has she been taught about customers? If you have arranged for someone to come a long way for a demonstration, wouldn't it be nice for them to feel welcomed from the start? A note to the receptionist saying, 'Mr A and Miss B from Bloxwich Packaging are coming – be specially nice to them,' may ensure your visitors feel special from the start, not intruders. If your receptionist has not been trained, then you can help her, and yourself.

Fred: First-rate machine, very popular, clear, quick and simple to operate. Any fool can work one. It's very simple . . . copy something. Good idea.

Freds never bother to prepare. But preparation is vital if the demonstration is to go smoothly. Of course you should find out as much as possible beforehand, to help you prepare.

Basil (*on the phone*): I think it would be very helpful if you could come over and see the range.
Customer: I could make it on Friday morning, at about ten.
Basil: Fine. Now, you're really only interested in semi-automatic equipment, aren't you?
Customer: Yes, our batch sizes don't lend themselves to fully automatic. It's a question of unit cost, though.
Basil: How about cycle-time?
Customer: Well, as you know the B35s average twenty a minute, but down-time seems to be increasing.
Basil: I think we can show you quite an improvement on both those factors on Friday.

Sometimes, though, you can't get prior warning. Then you just have to be prepared for any possibility.

Here is Ann, who sells electric blenders.

Customer: But I could have done that mixture pretty well with a hand whisk.
Ann: Would you like to try with pastry?
Customer: Does it do pastry?
Ann: I'll just fix the pastry hooks.

So, before the demonstration check with other people involved that you have all the equipment you need, and find out as much as you can about the customer's requirements. Try out the equipment, and rehearse. You're putting on a show! You have to be word perfect and action perfect or you'll let the production down. In other words, *don't take chances.*

Now, Act Two. **During the demonstration** there are four golden rules for you to remember. Let's see the first one being broken.

Fred (*operating the machine*): The 2300 is a fully automated electrostatic copier operating with conventional oxide-coated paper . . .

Fred doesn't know that you must keep quiet while the customer is watching the demonstration. You talk before it, and you talk after it, but you don't talk while you're showing it, because if you do, either he won't take in what you're showing him, or he won't take in what you're telling him.

At a photographic counter . . .

Fred: Then you just press this one to tighten the shot and this one to widen it. Would you like to look? As you can see, with the telephoto converter's side angle you can increase to a range from 6.5 to 78mm. And the slow-motion features make panning shots possible where otherwise you'd need a tripod, and with the automatic exposure you always get the optimum aperture setting even if the exposure actually changes during the shot and the manual override . . .

Customer: I'm sorry, what did you say?

Fred: I was just telling you . . .

When to talk

If people knew when to shut up, the history of our species would be quite different. In selling there is a time to ask questions. That's while you are establishing the customer's needs and countering his objections. There are two occasions when you need to be silent. The first is when he is examining your product. The second is when you have closed the sale.

That's golden rule number one – tell, show, tell.

The second golden rule is to show respect for the equipment. If you don't, how can the customer? The customer will judge the product's value by your attitude to it. Simple?

Show respect for the equipment.

But it works. Now let's move on to golden rule number three – get the customer to handle the equipment. Remember Fred in the photocopier showroom?

Customer: I see. Can I work it myself?
Fred: You can if you want to, but *you* won't be using it, will you?

Even when the customer suggested it (which they don't usually), Fred failed to give him the chance to try out the machine for himself. Normally, the demonstrator has to create the opportunity for the customer to try out the equipment.

Ann: . . . So you can see, with this hairdryer, you can have both hands free for sewing or knitting, say.

Customer: That's a good idea.

Ann: Another useful feature is that by turning this dial you can adjust the temperature . . . a quick, easy adjustment to the heat you want. You try it.

Customer: I see. It's cooler now. That's very good. The children often complain that our dryer's too hot.

Ann: No trouble with this.

So there are three of the golden rules:

1 Tell, show, tell.
2 Handle the equipment with respect.
3 Make the customer try out the product.

And the fourth? Well, let's see what other mistakes Fred made.

Customer: I wonder what would happen if we . . .

Fred: It's pretty self-explanatory, really, isn't it? Any other model I can show you?

Customer: No. It was just the 2300 I wanted to see.

Fred: Good, well, there it is.

Customer: Yes . . .

Fred: So that's it, then. Very nice to meet you.

Three times Fred failed to get the customer to ask questions. Three times he just didn't bother to find out whether the customer had any doubts . . . or what they were. Just think of it from the customers' point of view. Why are they watching your demonstration? So that you can prove the product is the one they need. And at any stage they may have doubts. If those doubts are not dealt with they won't buy the product. So you've got to ask

Don't show your training

The best sales training is not visible. A salesperson who is too obviously parroting some pre-arranged spiel will soon be caught out. You need to be responsive to different kinds of customer, and different customer's needs. Most of these customers will feel happier dealing with a human being, not a talking manual.

questions to get them to bring their doubts into the open. Let's watch Ann demonstrating a refrigerator.

Ann: With this model you never need to take the food out. The temperature inside stays the same even while it's defrosting. It's controlled by this thermostat.
Customer: Oh, I see. You needn't take everything out, then?
Ann: That's right. But I can see that you're still not quite happy about it.
Customer: What happens to the water?
Ann: When it defrosts?
Customer: Yes. Where does it go?
Ann: It evaporates. You don't have to drain it off – it happens automatically.
Customer: In the kitchen?
Ann: Yes.
Customer: Doesn't it get rather steamy?
Ann: It isn't very much. You hardly notice it.
Customer: I see.
Ann: Anything else?
Customer: No. I understand that now.

Only now can Ann go on to the next point that she wants to prove. It can be a slow process uncovering those doubts, but you've got to if you're going to succeed. So get the customer to ask questions. That is the fourth golden rule to remember when you are actually giving a demonstration.

Now finally – the Third Act – **After**. It's pretty simple – don't kick your customer straight out.

Fred: Good, well, there it is.
Customer: Yes . . .
Fred: That's it, then. Very nice to meet you.

Talk it over. Find out whether he's still got any doubts. You won't make a sale if he has . . .

Basil: How did that performance compare with your own experience?
Customer: Overall, you seem to show a 20 per cent improvement but . . . let's face it, I'm not sure our operators would do so well.
Basil: Well, let me show you the output figures that Moorfields achieved just one month after they changed over.

Keep digging for doubts till you're sure your points have been accepted.

Now your customer needs a hand-out. Any literature, illustrations, performance figures, anything that reminds him of the sales points you've made and the information you've given him.

Basil: Finally, here's the comparison between this new model and the equipment you've got at present.
Customer: Oh.

That's what the demonstration's for.

Basil: So, to sum up – your two questions were basically about quality and unit cost. Do you feel happy with what you've seen today?
Customer: Yes. You covered everything very fully.
Basil: Then I take it we can go ahead?
Customer: Yes . . . why not?

And even if you can't get an order there and then, at least get a commitment to the next step towards it. So that's the Third Act of your performance – after the demonstration. Talk it over, keep digging for doubts and give him the hand-outs to remind him of every-

The hand-out

The hand-out is rarely written by salesmen. Sometimes it is very good. At its worst, it is very bad. Like bad showrooms, you should not tolerate bad, or late, promotional material. It is a vital sales support, and to suffer the lack of it in silence is to make yourself responsible for the lost sales. If it affects your job, it's no good saying 'It's not my job' – especially if you are someone expected to display aggression and drive. Many companies skimp the promotional aids: if yours is one, make sure that your complaints are audible. Otherwise you are like a soldier with insufficient bullets. If necessary, have a go at rewriting it yourself, with the customer's needs in mind.

thing you've told him. Try to close the sale, or at least get a commitment.

Now that we've rehearsed all the scenes let's watch the whole show. First, **before** – the why and the preparation.

Customer: It's not really a question of machinery, it's a question of people.

Basil: Tell me, do you mean quantity of people, or quality?

Customer: Frankly, both. We're fairly small, so improved output by our staff would help a lot . . . apart from that, finding staff for our kind of quality work gets harder every day.

Basil: Then I think I can show you a machine to solve your people problem.

(*Bearing this in mind, Basil confers with his colleagues.*)

Basil: We've got to prove to him that we can speed up his output and that the machine's easy to operate. He's got problems getting skilled staff, you know – it's high quality work.

Doug: You can show him that it's easy enough, and he can try it for himself.

Basil: Yes. I was thinking . . . let's have one of your young lads standing around and I'll get him to use it.

Doug: Young Nicholls here has used one.

Basil: OK, we'll give him a quick run-through. I'll meet Clegg in reception at three and I'll bring him in here about a quarter past three after the chat. What material have we got for him to work on?

Doug: Georgian window frames.

Basil: Better have some laminated board and hardwood too.

Doug: Drawer side or worktops?

Basil: A mixture. He mustn't think we've

rigged it for soft wood or anything. I assume we've got a spare machine on standby?

Doug: As usual. Not that we've had a breakdown yet.

Basil: Always a first time. Right! Let's have a go then.

Basil: Mains on. Have you tightened the chuck?

Doug: Yes, and we've got a selection of bits.

Basil: You can't say I don't try to catch you out. Right, Nicholls, away you go. Remember, when I give it to you, handle it like the Crown Jewels, OK? Now, let's double-check everything – the display, the range of accessories, examples of the work they all do, and the spare tools.

So that's Act One

For Act Two – **during the demonstration** – let's change the scene. After all, the rules of demonstrating apply to every product. Ann's already found out **why**, and she's done her preparation. So she's going to **tell, show and tell**, and **handle the product with respect**.

Ann: Each drawer slides on plastic-coated runners, so it has a light, easy action and it's no trouble to open even when the drawers are full . . . very smooth.

Customer: I see.

Ann: And there are nylon buffers at the end so that it always closes neatly and quietly, with hardly any sound.

Customer: Could I pull a drawer right out by accident?

Ann: No. These arms are very strong. I'll pull it quite hard. You're perfectly safe. All right?

Customer: Yes.

Ann: These rails are also coated with
plastic, so that the ends of these
pockets, which are nylon, also run
smoothly, which helps if any of the files
are very heavy, like this one. You can
also run through the files without that
awful noise you get with metal on metal.
Customer: That's good. I work in the
waiting room, so . . .

These are the first two rules to remember
during the demonstration. And the other
two? . . . **Get the customer to handle the
product** and **encourage him to ask questions.**

No, no, sir – the *machine*,
handle the *machine*!

Get the customer to handle the product.

Basil: Try it yourself.
Customer: Thank you. First I press this . . .
Basil: That's right.
Customer: And then put this in . . . like this?
Basil: Fine. It's loaded now.
Customer: And it doesn't matter which way I put it in?
Basil: There's no problem. It will only fit one way.
Customer: Goon-proof.
Basil: Just about. Now you've loaded it, and you want to see it on the screen. Let me show you.

So that's the Second Act – during the demonstration.

Now for the Third Act – **after**.

Basil: We're trying to do two things with that router you've seen – increase output and meet your needs for quality. What do you think?
Customer: Six would cost a lot of money.
Basil: I think you'll find the savings more than make up for that.
Customer: Damn near every salesman I've ever met has told me that one.
Basil: Supposing the users told you?
Customer: Such as?
Basil: Arthur Duckworth. Geoff Jacobs at Bowles and Barton. Bob Harris . . .
Customer: Bob Harris? I didn't know he used them.
Basil: Why not ask him about his costs?
Customer: Yes, I'll give him a ring.
Basil: Now we can look at quality . . .

So, after the demonstration, talk it over. Dig out any lingering doubts the customer might have. Next, give the customer any relevant literature.

Basil: You'll find all the things I've shown you in here. And there's a list of the other accessories which allow you to develop it later.

Give the customer anything that will remind him of the points you've proved, and then – the whole point of the demonstration – try to make a sale.

Ann: That really seems to suit your needs, doesn't it?
Customer: Yes, I'm sure it will.
Ann: Splendid. Our van delivers in your area on Friday. Will that be all right?
Customer: I shall have to check with the doctors first.
Ann: About the price?
Customer: I'm afraid so.
Ann: I'm sure they'll agree. I know what . . . if I call you on Thursday morning we can just make the Friday van.
Customer: That's fine. But please wait until ten-thirty, when the surgery's over.
Ann: Of course, I'll make a note to ring you at eleven.

So, if you can make a sale, do so. If not, get a commitment to the next step in making that sale.

Closing the order

If the customer has come to see you, or if, perhaps after previous discussion, you have brought the product for the customer to assess, it's probably time to close the sale. You're the salesman, you're supposed to be the pushy one, so almost certainly the customer is waiting for you to make the move. If you don't, he'll escape, feeling relieved, because another salesman is coming to see him tomorrow with a competitive product.

So, ask for the order.

Before the demonstration find out why you're giving it, and prepare.

Don't talk while you're actually giving the demonstration – tell, show, tell.

Handle the product with respect.

Get the customer to try out the product.

Encourage him to ask questions.

After the demonstration keep digging for doubts.

Reinforce the demonstration with sales aids and give him the hand-outs.

Close the sale.

Golden rules

Here you are, guv' – all you ever wanted to know about buying cold-rolled sections from Atkinson & Mudge, but were afraid to ask.

Nobody reads things that look like hard work, and are of no direct concern to them.

French: Thank you very much for coming to see me.

Moore: It's my pleasure.

French: And I really like the sound of that 47B.

Moore: Yes, that's certainly the one you need.

French: I'm sure it is. Good, well send me the details and set the wheels in motion, as they say, and we'll ... er ...

Moore: That's fine, Mr French, thank you for the time you've given up.

6 The proposal

There comes a moment in every young salesman's life when he has made a convincing sales presentation and overcome the customer's initial objections. He then finds himself asked to submit a written proposal – and that's where many a promising man comes unstuck.

The salesman in this case is Peter Moore, a Sales Engineer. He covers a large territory for a company called Parker and Gibbs. He's responsible for bringing into his company all the profitable business in his area. It's a big job, and it costs Parker and Gibbs a lot of money – one way and another – just for the chance of a sale. Like the chance he now has with Mr French.

Moore and French have gone through a survey, and they think they are all set for a sale which will benefit them both. The question is, will Peter be able to bring it off?

He has now returned to his own office and summoned his secretary.

Moore: Penny, come in here and bring your notebook with you, would you? I've sold a 47B.

Penny: Are you *sure* you've really sold it?

Moore: Oh yes, it's in the bag this time. Ready? To John French at Barnthorpe and Co. Dear sir, the writer wishes to thank you for the courtesy extended to

*So you think
you can sell?*

The salesperson's letter

Many a persuasive salesperson falls down on his letters. Yet these should be easier: no customer to cope with, ample time to consider what to say. Don't be afraid of the written word. Let your letters reflect your own style and personality so that you present a uniform appearance to your customer.

If in doubt, try the FOG Index. Devised by James Gunning, it's designed to test the obscurity of the written word. From a sample of 100 words or more, divide the number of words by the number of sentences to find the average number of words per sentence. Then count the number of words with three or more syllables (omitting proper names, words like tape-recorder, and verb endings like -ing). Add the average number of words per sentence to the total number of long words, and multiply by 0.4. If you come out between 9–12 on the FOG Index you are a reasonably clear communicator. If you exceed 12, you need to change your approach.

him during his visit . . . or should we say on the occasion of his visit?

Penny: Just keep going – I can do this bit backwards.

Moore: . . . visit on Thursday 11 September. As requested, we attach our quotation for one ParGibb 47B, and look forward in due course to the esteemed favour of your instructions. We assure you of our very best attention at all times and remain . . . and so on. Right, now the quotation itself. Usual form with the exclusions on the back. Get the number from the file . . . We have pleasure in quoting for your requirements as follows:

1 Supply hopper with lid.
2 Alternative for dual auto-feed.
3 Cruciform frame, double enamelled and weld-tested.
4 Grovelling head, milled teeth and bearings as standard.
5 Reversing attachment and actuator . . . the whole subject to our standard conditions: £1274.53, excluding VAT, installation and commissioning. Note that delivery depends upon conditions ruling.

Right, do that right away, Penny.

Penny: Okay. By the way, I've been meaning to ask you . . . what exactly is a 47B?

Moore: Don't you ever listen when you take dictation?

Penny: Yes, but what does it . . . ?

Moore: Send that off as soon as you've typed it, would you? Mr French is waiting for it.

Peter Moore, pleased with a job that he thinks he has done well, sits back and dreams of the scene when Mr French receives his mail the next day.

Sue: I knew you would want to open this
yourself.

French: Oh yes, it's from that clever
young Mr Moore at Parker and Gibbs.
Aha! . . . auto-feed 432 . . . grovelling
head plus milled teeth and bearings . . .
ParGibbs mark two fondallators . . .
The whole thing only costs £1274.53
plus VAT. We must have it, Sue. We
must.

Both: We must! We must!

French: Ooh, I can't wait to see all those
exciting components . . .

Is that what will really happen? Really? This
is probably more like it.

Sue: Do you feel able to look at the post?

French: All right. A circular . . . a bill . . .
final demand . . . 'giant carpet sale' . . .
What's this? Ah . . . from Moore . . .
Tell me, Sue, who teaches people to
write rubbish like 'look forward in due
course to the esteemed favour of your
instructions'? Garbage! Grovelling head!
Actuator! £1274.53? Plus VAT, plus
installation and commissioning? Good
God.

Sue: Would you like me to file it for you,
Mr French?

French: More reasons on the back why
they won't sell it to me than reasons on
the front for buying it. In fact, there
aren't many reasons for buying it.

A much more likely reaction.

Moore's mistake was to send a quotation,
when what French really wanted (when he
said 'send me the details') was a proposal.

A quotation is just a pile of jargon with a
price at the end, and you don't need it until
after the customer's agreed to buy. It forms
the basis of a legal contract, and really just
tells the client how much he has to pay out –

If in doubt, clarify

Not everyone means the same
thing by certain words and
phrases. Peter Moore thought he
had an order. 'I like it' doesn't
mean 'I'll buy it'. Make sure you
know the difference between a
quotation and a proposal, and can
set out either in plain English.

that's bound to put anyone off.

A proposal would give him a presentation of the reasoning behind the sale – the reasons why he should say yes. The benefits, the attractions, the savings . . .

So why not have a go at producing a proposal, Peter?

Moore: Penny, forget about that
　　quotation, we don't want it.
Penny: I've just typed it.
Moore: Well, I'm doing something
　　different now. I'm writing a proposal.
Penny: Shall I get my note pad?
Moore: No, just get me some coffee.
　　Let's see . . . benefits, attractions,
　　savings . . .

Throughout the afternoon and into the evening Moore slaves away, labouring over the proposal. He carries on throughout the night. As dawn breaks he is nearing the end, and by the time Penny arrives in the office he has just finished. With a manic gleam in his eye, he points out to her a huge pile of paper.

Moore: Type that!
Penny: All of it?
Moore: All of it.
Penny: Are you sure?
Moore: Course I'm sure.
Penny: You're not going to change your
　　mind *after* I've typed it?
Moore: Certainly not. It's all there. This
　　is the 47B. There's nothing more to be
　　said.
Penny: But even when I've typed it, it will
　　be at least forty-five pages.
Moore: Well . . . compress it a bit, okay?

His mammoth task completed, Peter again envisages the scene when Mr French receives the proposal.

Sue: I think it's a proposal for the 47B.

French: It's come!

Penny: I brought it straight to you.

French: Open it quickly, let me see it.
It's so big! So thorough, so
comprehensive. I'll read it straight away.
Cancel everything . . . no telephone calls
or interruptions of any kind. And cancel
that lunch with the chairman. Oooh, I
do like a good read.

Sue: Do you think you'll finish it today?

French: Well, if I haven't finished it by
the time I go home, I'll sit up all night
and read it in bed.

Of course it wouldn't really be like that.

French: What on earth's that?

Sue: It's all right, it's been through
security.

*(They approach it with caution. French
struggles with the sellotape and string, and
finally manages to tear it apart.)*

French: It's from Parker and Gibbs. A
proposal.

Sue: Good grief, fancy having to type all
that.

French: Fancy having to read it.

Sue: Well, you certainly can't this
morning. I've got two calls holding for
you already, there's the Executive
Committee at ten-thirty and then you've
got the chairman's lunch followed
by . . .

French: Let's look at the diary. Dublin
. . . Zurich . . . how about 2 August?

Sue: Shall I file it for you, Mr French?

Of course, it might be even worse.

Sue: Won't you just have a look at it first?

French: No. Tell you what, though. Get

Buying signals

Some manuals for salespeople may make selling seem more like British Rail. Customers, unfortunately, do not turn on green lights to say, 'I am ready to buy.' Nevertheless, the skilful salesperson is alert to the half-involuntary gestures that help to define the customer's position. 'That's most impressive', or 'I really think this line could catch on', or 'With that weight of promotion, it's hard to ignore' – all these and similar utterances are an invitation to the salesperson to close, and close confidently. Sometimes the signal is less clear: a double yellow, not a green. 'This could be good, but will it really knock out the brand leaders?' or 'What if Mr Famous Person doesn't plug it on TV?' – such signals invite the well-prepared salesperson to give the customer more confidence to buy. The signal can be against you. 'People in Beaconsfield don't want this sort of thing,' or 'It's wrong for the North. Peanut butter never did well up here.' This above all is a vital signal – to make a sale you are going to have to use all the skills this book covers.

hold of old Briggs from our other people, you know – Universal International. He'll be glad to read it. And he's a straight enough chap, he'll tell me what it really means – and he might come up with a better idea.

French will not be in the least tempted to read a proposal that is forty-five pages long. It will be a chore, and it's completely impersonal. Nobody reads things that look like hard work, and are of no direct concern to their interests or problems.

Peter Moore should have written a sales case for the customer, not a product blast for himself. Nobody ever buys a 47B, or whatever it is – they buy what it would do for them. So what you must do is present a brief, attractive sales case, written for the individual customer. Since customers buy for different reasons, the selling case is always slightly different. You can't make a move in selling until you know why the customer is buying.

For example, French told Moore during their meeting that he wanted to use less skilled labour and keep his operating costs down to ten pence per component. So, bearing this in mind, the first thing for Peter to remember when planning his proposal is to state the objectives of the sale; that is, to list the particular objectives that the customer wants to achieve from buying the product.

Then you simply have to prove that what you are selling will achieve these objectives for him. Save the rest of your product's virtues for later. At this stage, just compare what the customer does now with what you can do to improve things for him. Show him that the 47B can do what you say it can do.

The 47B will enable Mr French to cut his labour costs by half. So Peter should say so, and prove it, with facts and figures.

At least we double-glazed your eyes,
you miserable old git.

*The skilful salesman is alert to the half-involuntary gestures
that help define the customer's position.*

Then you can tell the customer all the benefits that come if he buys the product. For example, that the 47B is smaller, more mobile, has more flexibility, reduces errors by 20 per cent and cuts capital outlay.

Next, you should give the financial justification. Not just the price, but the proof of how much you save from the day you install a 47B. How little it costs, over a period. You're certainly not trying to hide the price. On the contrary, when you give the financial justification it's your big moment. You can tell the customer about your leasing terms or hire purchase, and his total savings set off against the investment in the machine. This is when you make the customer see that he can't afford *not* to buy.

And one last point. You must sell the backing that you give. After all, no product is any better than your ability to keep it working.

So now, let's give Peter another chance to write a proposal.

Moore: Penny! Er, Penny? . . . Do you think you could type this proposal and send it off to Mr French?

Penny: What, another one? This is the last time, okay?

Moore: Oh it is, it is. At least it's smaller this time.

Yet again, Peter dreams of the reception of his proposal.

French: . . . And here are the very two points which really determine whether or not we should buy this. Performance figures comparing our 33C with the 47B – details of the lubrication system that will really solve that down-time problem. And the price – all worked out per shift – and leasing terms too. I shall write out a cheque straight away. Ee, this is a grand day for Barnthorpe's.

Why don't you stop daydreaming, Peter Moore? You *know* that nobody ever writes out a cheque as soon as they receive a proposal. Let's face up to all the other things that might happen.

French: Since I spoke to old George, we seem to need something a bit different.
or
French: Thing is, Briggs from Universal popped in yesterday and I was quite impressed with his new machine.
or
French: When I mentioned it to old Alf in Production he didn't think we needed one yet.
or
French: I've just been told the Financial Meeting's off – all capital expenditure's

being reviewed.

Sue: I'm sorry, Mr French, you seemed so pleased with it.

French: I was, but things have changed.

Sue: Shall I file it for you, Mr French?

Now, if Peter had taken the proposal with him and presented it to the customer personally, he could have ironed out any problems as they arose. You must be selective, of course. You should only deliver the most important proposals yourself, the ones you can least afford to lose. After all, by the time a sale gets this far, both you and the company have a great deal tied up in it. Isn't it worth the effort to actually close the sale?

The typed proposal I promised you, sir — for the extra box of staples . . .

Only deliver the most important proposals yourself.

Don't rely on anything, apart from yourself

You're the salesperson. When you've closed the deal, it's done. Until then, it's a potential waste of time and money. If it's a big sale, don't rely on the post. A cannier competitor who's read the sales manuals too may be sitting in Mr French's office at this moment, subtly denigrating your machine and pressing the virtues of his company's similar machine. Don't assume, because you've got an interested buyer, that the sale is made.

So Peter is now going to take his proposal to French in person. Let's watch.

Moore: Thank you for seeing me so quickly, Mr French. I wanted to be absolutely sure that our proposal was what you wanted. If you remember, at our last meeting you felt that the two most significant items to you in considering new plant were, first – the use of less skilled labour, and second – operating costs, which you wanted to keep to less than ten pence per component. Do you still feel the same, or has anything come up to change your mind?

French: No, that's exactly what we'd like – if you can do it. But now our production manager tells me he thinks we need something adequate to 450 cps.

Moore: Well, that's all right, because when we come to the performance curves you'll see that we can take it up to 515 cps using alternative motor sets.

French: Right, good . . .

Moore: It works! It works! Yippee! Oh . . . er . . . terribly sorry . . . just talking to myself.

State the objective – clearly, concisely and always bearing the customer's needs in mind.

Prove you can meet the objective.

Summarise the benefits.

Justify the cost.

List guarantees and service arrangements.

Take the proposal to the customer personally, so that you can iron out any problems that might arise.

Golden rules

7 Negotiation

Negotiation

It puts you on the spot.

You can't negotiate without some power to take decisions. Make sure you know what your latitude is. Many a bad deal has been made because a salesman was flattered into agreeing something he shouldn't. It's a good rule to suggest your freedom of movement is more restricted than it really is. Then, take your time. Think through the customer's proposals and note them point by point.

Don't leave things hanging in the air. 'I thought we'd covered that' doesn't sound so good when the customer is demanding a huge credit note. The small print is usually there for a reason: make it your reason.

Many supplier/buyer situations, which we have traditionally viewed as 'selling' relationships, have changed significantly during the last ten years or so. During that time many major customers and agencies have develped their own expertise and their own commercial strategies, and are just as sophisticated as the major manufacturers. Some of them, perhaps, are even more advanced. Certainly some are more powerful. Recently there has been a considerable and growing concentration of buying power into a few hands.

These developments have meant that there is an increased amount of interdependence between suppliers and customers. Although the two sides still occasionally make independent warlike noises, there is tacit agreement that each side needs the other if they are to achieve their individual objectives. This means that most of the time, the need to buy and the need to sell are more or less equal. This in turn means less emphasis on 'selling' and more on negotiation. Let's look at the difference between the two.

When he is selling, the salesperson does not change his position. He induces the buyer to move towards him by heightening the buyer's perception of his need for the goods or service. In other words, he makes his customer want the product enough to think about buying it. The customer then turns his attention to the terms and conditions surrounding sale and purchase, and this is when negotiation takes over. Having been satisfied during the selling process that he can actively consider purchasing, he will now be seeking the best possible deal in a number of detailed areas – the actual price (including credit, discounts, etc), the exact specifications and allied services (including training, delivery and servicing).

Negotiation, therefore, is the give-and-take process whereby the final, detailed terms and conditions surrounding the purchase/supply decision are agreed. In this negotiation the supplier is tailoring the details of the marketing mix (product, price, presentation) to fit the local, immediate needs of one particular customer.

Because of this both the supplier and the purchaser are involved in controlled compromise.

Let's look at John Edmonds, an experienced salesman who is now embarking on his first major negotiation, over a contract for ten motorway machines . . .

Edmonds: Well, Mr Johnson, I hope you found our quotation satisfactory.

Johnson: It's interesting. Satisfactory is another matter. It's not as good as some of the others I received.

Edmonds: I'm sorry to hear that.

Johnson: It's all right technically. You've obviously understood our technical requirements, there's no quibble there. But what it doesn't make sufficient allowance for is that we're purchasing a total system here, not just a machine. It's the whole package, all the bits and pieces that go with it, that'll take some examining.

Johnson has put Edmonds under pressure right from the start, by bringing up competitive quotes and suggesting that he hadn't considered the 'package'.

And Edmonds fell for it. He immediately began apologising and conciliating – in other words, retreating. The trouble is that once you've traded down, it's quite a job to trade up again. In the early stages you must maintain neutrality. If a potential buyer does open a negotiation by giving you flak, you can absorb it by simply jotting down notes. It's a way of saying, 'Look, I'm paying attention, but I'm not committing myself.'

Are you a smoker?

Do you smoke if your customer doesn't? If the door says YOU ARE ENTERING A NO-SMOKING AREA, don't even ask. If unsure, ask by offering a cigarette and watch carefully when you say, 'Well, do you mind if I do?' If he'd clearly prefer you not to, even if saying 'yes', then don't. (You always meant to stop, or cut down, anyway.) If he is a smoker too, your offer of a cigarette, dexterity with lighter, etc., can help you to create the right atmosphere.

You're right – with these low-price speakers you could – aha – mistake Albinoni for the ice-cream van, but er – um . . .

Once you've traded down, it's quite a job to trade up again.

Edmonds: Well, would you like to be more specific, Mr Johnson? Let's see if there's any particular problem we can get out of the way.

Johnson: Here's one for starters . . . 'parts stock'. This quote specifies your recommended stock level for parts.

Edmonds: That's no more than our normal practice.

Johnson: But shouldn't you make some allowance for the fact that the ten machines we're buying are a brand-new model? Compared to standard models, the parts-stock level recommended for these works out much more expensive. It'll involve my company in considerable financial commitment.

Edmonds: Only in relative terms, surely.

Johnson: Relative or not, what it comes down to is tying up a lot of capital in something that might not even get used. Not only am I loath to commit that amount for something that's possibly unnecessary, I don't think it's a reasonable demand for you to make. Now, let me tell you what I think would work out much fairer to both sides.

That's a phrase to watch out for!

Johnson: Here's how we can cut through it. In those instances where your recommendations prove to have been over-estimated – where we find we haven't used all those spare parts during the first twelve months – is there any reason why you shouldn't agree to take back the unused parts, free of charge? Eh?

Edmonds: Well, we're really only talking about the 'C'-class spares, aren't we? The 'A'-class and 'B'-class parts you can use in your standard machines.

Johnson: Obviously it's only the 'C'-class parts that may wind up unused. And taking them back isn't going to present you with any difficulties, is it? For one thing, I think that warranty . . .

Edmonds: Well, that would take care of a proportion of them, yes.

Johnson: And all we're negotiating is the first twelve months. Now after that, if – as seems highly probable – I find myself buying more of these machines from you . . .

Edmonds: You'll be needing to balance up your parts stock. Well, I agree that shouldn't cost us very much – there shouldn't be any big problem. Yes, I'm sure we can produce a reasonable buy-back position there for you.

Dangerous phrases

'You scratch my back, I'll scratch
yours.'
  'We're nearly there, but . . .'
  'Just one or two minor points to
clear up.'
  'This would be to your
advantage.'
  'I'd have thought you could
easily manage . . .'
  'I don't want to seem to teach
you your business, but . . .'
  'Surely you could just . . .'

In exchange for nothing? And so early in the game? Even though it was a reasonable enough request, Edmonds should not have conceded it before he knew what else Johnson had on his shopping list. It doesn't matter how justified any objection may be. You should never make an offer on it till you've got the cost-list of everything he intends to argue with you about. This is an absolutely basic negotiating rule.

Then – equally basic – never give in on it (as Edmonds did with those parts) without trying to get something in return. Don't ever donate a concession, trade it. And even then, if you do decide to grant it, you've got to make it look as though it's hurting you. When Edmonds said, 'Well, that won't cost us very much,' it didn't even sound like a concession.

Johnson: If we're agreed on that, it looks
  like we're in business.

That's a phrase that should always make you nervous.

Johnson: As soon as we can clear up a
  couple of other minor points I think
  we've got ourselves a deal.

And so's that.

Edmonds: Great. So what are those
  minor points?
Johnson: Well, there's the question of
  delivery. Three of the vehicles can go to
  Birmingham as specified, but now we'd
  like the others to be delivered to our
  local depots. After talking it over with
  the regional managers, they'd now like
  to have the machines in their areas to
  see how they perform under different
  geographical conditions. From your
  point of view, of course, that can only
  be to the good, right? Another

advantage where you're concerned is that it gives us both the opportunity to find out the demand in particular areas – see perhaps where some extra machines might be needed.

Edmonds: It would entail extra delivery costs, though.

Johnson: But they'd only be minimal, surely. You're not telling me that you don't already deliver to London, Manchester, Glasgow and Plymouth?

Edmonds: It's hardly the same as delivering all ten to Birmingham.

Johnson: I am surprised to hear you say that.

Edmonds: Look, you must agree that you're asking for a pretty wide spread.

Johnson: I'm aware of the geography. What surprised me is that in the competitive quotes we've had, the companies concerned have offered free delivery to the depots.

Edmonds: I see. Well, in that case I'd better talk to our financial manager.

Edmonds has just fallen for a familiar con job. Not only did he swallow that pseudo-carrot about the regional managers buying extra machines, he also allowed himself to be beaten over the head with the rubber stick of the opposition's quote. This was just another example of the vital importance of having the whole package under your belt before getting into discussion on any individual concession.

The question of delivery often gives you considerable scope for manoeuvre, because there are so many 'variables' involved – time, place, cost, quantity – whatever you're forced to concede on one, you can generally claw back on another.

The word 'variables' is crucial to negotiating. You see, anything that the other side accepts as a 'constant' can nearly always be turned into a 'variable'.

127

Johnson: Now, as I see it, another point at issue is this provision you've made for operator training at your base in Wolverhampton.

Edmonds: 'A course for ten people – one per machine.' Again, that's standard practice.

Johnson: But are we in a standard situation? My new Director of Training thinks not. He says that as well as the operators, our fitters should have a chance to familiarise themselves with these new machines. So what we're really talking about is twenty to twenty-five people going for training.

Edmonds: I see. Well, I appreciate the value of that idea, of course, but it could somewhat overload our training school. We only schedule our programmes in accordance with the sales forecasts on the machine. So there'd be an immediate problem with lecturers, accommodation, courses – any number of things.

Johnson: So the question becomes, how can we best achieve this with minimum cost and inconvenience to you?

This is another 'red-light' phrase. He's not in business to save you money.

Edmonds: I'd have to try to work that one out.

Johnson: My new feller already has. If he pulls all our twenty to twenty-five people together at one of our depots – let's say Birmingham because that's closest to you – then we could lay on all the accommodation etcetera for ourselves. And all you'd have to provide would be one trainer and one machine. There you are, that takes the whole thing off your shoulders, doesn't it.

Edmonds: It's a thought.

Johnson: Well. Let's think about it. By any standards this is a large order we would be placing with you. And I know that your training programmes are attended by people from all sorts of other companies. I don't think it's wise to give our competitors the tip-off that we're going in for your new machines. So it would seem eminently reasonable that you allow us to keep all our people under our own roof, to maintain the necessary security over this order.

Edmonds: I'd have to check with my training centre to see if there's a demonstration machine available.

To give himself time to think, Edmonds could have called the training centre there and then, to find out whether a machine would be available. Even if he already knew the answer, it might have been a useful delaying tactic, enabling him to work out what the actual cost of those revised training arrangements would be. Then, of course, he would have to add that to the price of everything else he'd conceded. Better still, it would have been an opportunity for Edmonds to give the training provisions another run-through, mentally, to see whether anything else there could serve as a 'variable'. At the very least it might have slowed things down a bit. As it was, Johnson realised that he was on a winning streak. That's why he decided to clobber Edmonds with a final demand, for a discount.

Johnson: I think we're almost there. I'll tell you what does occur to me, though. Don't you have an arrangement with certain other companies whereby, after an agreed period of time, you agree to buy back their machines? I can't help feeling that because these new MCMs we'll be purchasing are an unknown

The marketing mix

This familiar phrase needs to be thoroughly understood. It embraces every negotiable aspect of the relationship between producer and customer:

- The product itself and its specification
- Its packaging or presentation
- Its publicity
- Its price
- Its quantity
- Its delivery arrangements
- The payment period
- The return or resale arrangements
- The clearance of existing products, about to be replaced
- The maintenance and service arrangements

quantity, we should have some such
buy-back deal here.

Edmonds: Oh no. I don't think my
company would agree to that, not with a
guaranteed price. These machines are
so new, no one could calculate with any
certainty what future demand levels for
them might be. Especially bearing in
mind the current economic situation.

Johnson: It's naming a buy-back price in
advance that creates a problem for you?

Edmonds: Exactly. I'm sure you see the
difficulty.

Johnson: Oh, I can see a difficulty, yes.
But what I hope I can also see is your
desire to find future business here. So
why don't we think around it? See if,
between us, we can't come up with
some alternative route for arriving at the
same point? Eh? Obviously I'm
disappointed that you find yourself
unable to offer me the facility of a
buy-back guarantee, but equally
obviously I do see that it might be
unfair to expect you to commit
yourselves to it.

Johnson has now made Edmonds feel guilty,
and shown what a reasonable bugger he
himself is.

Johnson: But to my mind, some kind of
discount on the quoted price might be
an equitable alternative.

Edmonds: Mr Johnson, the price we've
quoted is very keen. Although we'd very
much like to retain your custom, I really
don't think that price gives us a great
deal of leeway.

Johnson: There must be some, if only
because there were competitive quotes
which bettered it.

Edmonds: Well, what level of discount
are you talking about?

Johnson: What we have to remember about these new MCMs is that, whilst their performance has been tested, it still has to be proved over the long term. So, bearing in mind that long-term aspect, I'd say that something in the region of about 4½ per cent would be acceptable to me and would not be unfair to you.

Edmonds: Four and a half per cent!

Johnson: Aye!

Some time and some desperate haggling later . . .

Edmonds: Well, I'll take it back to my company if you like, but as far as I'm concerned, 2½ per cent is as far as we can go.

Johnson: I'll tell you what I'll do, then. You're sure that 2½ per cent is within your authority?

Edmonds: I'll have my hide tanned for it – but yes.

Johnson: Good lad. Right, then, let's recap the points we've agreed.

Edmonds has now completely lost control of the interview. He should have been giving Johnson *his* understanding of the deal, from his notes.

The question of a discount was certainly difficult to argue with. So Edmonds shouldn't have let him get as far as haggling over the amount of the discount. He should have shifted the ground completely and offered a variable from somewhere else. But if he had remembered the four negotiating commandments, Edmonds would not have got himself into this mess.

Can you do the unexpected?

If your negotiation is being bogged down in questions of tedious detail, it's an important aspect of control to be able to switch to another tack. Not an irrelevant one but one more likely to achieve your aim. Your customer may be relieved as well. Introduce a phrase like, 'I've been wondering whether . . .' or even, 'On a totally different topic . . .' and return to the previous subject when you feel you can control it more effectively. Don't do this too often, though.

The four negotiating commandments:

1 Aim high.
2 Get the other fellow's total shopping list before you start arguing.
3 Keep the whole package in mind all the time.
4 Keep searching for variables.

Now, bearing in mind these commandments, let's look at how Edmonds should have handled the interview. The best possible deal would be for Johnson to accept the quotation exactly as it stands. So that's where Edmonds should start.

Edmonds: Well, Mr Johnson, now you've had a chance to study our quotation, I'm hoping we can reach a decision today. There's such a heavy demand on these new machines, any delay could set back delivery fairly seriously, I'm afraid.

Johnson: Oh, I see no reason at all why we shouldn't reach an agreement today. There's not much to quarrel about. Our technical people are happy about the machine itself – so all you and I have to do is talk over a few points like getting the machines in, developing the staff and so on. The areas, in other words, where your company – and I'll say it frankly – is a little weak as compared to some competitive quotes.

Edmonds: You needn't tell me, Mr Johnson. We know how worried our competitors are. So by all means let's get those little matters out of the way first. If you tell me which ones are causing you concern, then perhaps we can consider the whole thing together.

Johnson: Well . . . some of them I'd hardly call little points. In fact, where my company is concerned, they're of quite major importance.

Edmonds: What areas are they?

Johnson: Well, take this one. Finance. This recommended parts stock you've got here. Now, I understand why it is higher in volume and value than for a standard machine, but as far as we're concerned it represents a higher financial commitment than we're prepared to accept. So I think we should start by discussing ways and means of reducing that commitment.

Edmonds: Yes, we can certainly talk about that. What are the other points you put down for discussion?

Johnson: Never mind the others. I'd like your suggestions on the recommended parts stock.

Edmonds: Ah.

Johnson: After all, you were the one who brought up the importance of coming to a decision today. All right, let's get the parts stock recommendation out of the way and then we can steam ahead.

Edmonds: Very well then, Mr Johnson, if that's what you insist on.

When you're thrown, give yourself time to think.

Edmonds: But since it's something we'll need to go into in some detail, let me just do some sums . . .

(*He gets out his calculator.*)

Yes. The only thing is – for you to obtain the best possible concession out of it – we may need to tie into the total package. For instance, didn't you mention the matter of getting the machines in?

Johnson: Yes, I have got a point to raise about that . . .

Edmonds: Then it might help the parts stock area if we cost out those two in conjunction. What specific delivery

I've done some calculations which I think will prove the point —
but they're on a beer mat in the pub down the road.

When you're thrown, give yourself time to think.

query did you have in mind?

Johnson: Well, you've based these figures on the idea that all the machines are being delivered to Birmingham. But suppose three went to Birmingham, three to London, two to Manchester, one to Glasgow and one to Plymouth. Now, I imagine from your point of view delivery to these centres wouldn't present any major financial problem?

Edmonds (*calculating*): I'm just costing it out. Yes, I'm pretty sure that we can do something to help you there. . . . Is there anything else that represents a significant departure from the quotation?

Johnson: Well, one other thing, though I hardly think it merits the word significant. I happen to know that a lot of your customers have an agreed buy-back arrangement on your machines.

Edmonds: On the standard machines, yes, not on these new MCMs.

Johnson: Possibly that's because no one else has bought them in the quantity that we're taking.

Edmonds: No, that's true.

Johnson: In which case, I'd like to come to some agreement as to the level at which you'd be prepared to take these back, say after ten years' use.

Edmonds: A buy-back arrangement. So, have we now covered all the points at issue?

Johnson: Yes, I think we can say we have. So once we've settled those, then apart from a few minor details . . .

('Minor details' is a phrase that should make your blood run cold.)

Johnson: . . . we're in business.

Edmonds: Well, let's put these minor details on the list as well, once we're about it, shall we?

Johnson: There's just a little point about training. I don't see why we need to pay for your training course when it could be done at our depot.

Edmonds: I see. Well, let's start on the parts stock then.

Johnson: Well, what worries me is that there are the slow movers – the 'C'-class spares. Now there is no problem with the 'A'- and 'B'-class spares, because they're common to other machines, but I don't want to be landed with lots of 'C'-class spares I've no occasion to use. So what I'm proposing is an agreement from you that you will take back any unused 'C'-class parts free of charge.

Edmonds: Let's see what we can do in that direction . . . I think I can see a way through it. Now, although this quotation specifies that you take the total recommended stock of 'C'-class parts, it doesn't ask you to lay in the complete quantity of 'A'- and 'B'-class spares for the new machines.

Johnson: Obviously not. Because I already hold a certain number of 'A' and 'B' spares for my other machines.

Edmonds: Yes, which is why our quote only asks you to make up any shortfall between what you're already holding and the recommended 'A' and 'B' stock. So how about this suggestion; if you'll agree to take from us the total 'A' and 'B' stock recommended for the new machine, then I'm sure my people will agree a buy-back on however many 'C'-class spares remain unused after twelve months.

Johnson: Buy in all the 'A' and 'B' spares?

Edmonds: Well, you said yourself they can be used for any standard machines. So you're not likely to be left with any of those on your hands. There's always a use for things like basic split pins.

Johnson: Yes, that's right. Fair enough.

Edmonds: Well, let's make a note of that for the re-draft, shall we? Of course, what I'm hoping will happen a year from now is that you'll want to keep those 'C'-class spares – to maintain the additional MCMs you'll be buying.

Johnson: That's as may be. For today, I just want to get the arrangements on these ten right.

Edmonds: Okay. Let's move on, then. To that new set of delivery requirements you just sprang on me.

Johnson: The reason I mentioned those 'new' delivery requirements, as you call them, is because yours is not the only machine on the market. And the significant difference between your quote and those I've had from your competitors is that all of them are quite willing to deliver the machinery to our regional centres free of charge.

Don't create a winner/loser set-up.

Edmonds: No, of course, Mr Johnson, that's perfectly fair. But let me tell you why those delivery charges trouble me. Obviously I now have to take into account the fact that our competitors have offered you a wider spread of delivery – though I've a shrewd idea that's only because the demand for MCMs is now so great they've been forced into making all sorts of counter-offers – but the big problem it raises with us is low-loaders. Now I'd hazard a guess that your experience with low-loaders is probably even greater than ours.

Johnson: Aye, there's not much you can tell me about those damn things.

Edmonds: No, I wouldn't try. But what I would like to try and do is benefit from your knowledge of them by trying to see if there's a way of achieving that delivery spread you want on a basis of pooling our low-loader capacities.

Johnson: How would that help me? I'd just be cutting down your costs.

Edmonds: Not necessarily. Suppose, for example, you collected the MCMs yourself, which you could do quite simply with your Plymouth loader taking two and dropping one in London and your Glasgow loader taking two and dropping one in Birmingham. In that case we could completely remove the delivery charge from our cost. That would be a difference of about 0.75 per cent but it could be 1 per cent.

Johnson: Between 0.7 and 1 per cent, eh?

Body language

Your customer may have been trained to negotiate. He's watching your body language. Watch his. Why is he tapping his fingers? What does it mean when she leans back in her chair and presses her fingertips together? A listless air, failure to meet your eyes, nervous gestures – these are danger signals – the buyer has decided against, or has lost interest.

137

Give him a choice. Let him feel he's in control.

Edmonds: Or, if you take the other problem with low-loaders, capacity. Now I doubt if we could actually deal with so many locations all at once. So another alternative presents itself. Suppose we delay some of the delivery? Spread it out so that it's not completed till the end of January or the beginning of February? That way we could offer you a reduced delivery charge.

Johnson: Reduced by how much?

Edmonds: Well, not as much as the first alternative, obviously. Somewhere around 0.5 per cent, I should think. But it's a question of what suits you best. If you have low-loaders running light, as I imagine you would have at this time of year, I should think the first suggestion would suit you best. Besides which, that way you'd get the machines on the ground sooner, which would certainly put you ahead of the game.

Johnson: No, I think I prefer the second course. If you'll deliver at a reduced rate of not less than 0.5 per cent, I'd be prepared to accept the machines towards the end of January. Not February, though.

Edmonds: Right . . .

Johnson: Of course, these changes in your production schedule arising out of my agreement to the altered delivery arrangements – they do raise a point in regard to terms of payment.

Edmonds: Terms of payment? But they've already been agreed. Fifty per cent on acceptance of the quotation . . . 50 per cent on delivery of the machines.

Johnson: . . . some of which will not be delivered till the end of January.

Edmonds: But your written acceptance of

the quotation will still involve us in an immediate commitment of materials and skilled labour.

Johnson: I appreciate that. But you surely can't expect my company to tie its money up unnecessarily. So what I would like to propose is: instead of the 50 per cent deposit arrangements we will pay in full for each machine as it's delivered. You can see how that will solve our problem, and where you're concerned, well, the way you'll benefit is obvious.

That's not what he is in business for.

Johnson: You won't have to wait so long for our payment of the final 50 per cents.

Edmonds: Mr Johnson, what you're asking me to agree is . . .

(When you desperately need a delaying tactic, a phone call is one of the best.)

Edmonds: . . . a serious policy question. So serious I'll have to take advice on it from our machine-scheduling people. May I use the phone?

Johnson: This one's an outside line.

Edmonds: Are there any other points, apart from those we still have to deal with, that you'd like to raise?

Johnson: No, I don't think so.

Edmonds: Extension 36, please. Hallo, Edmonds here. Is Harry Gascoigne about, please?

Oh . . . very well, when will he be back? I see, I'll ring again.

He'll be back in a few minutes. Look, I'll tell you what – let's leave that one until I can get hold of him – and so as not to waste time, let's move on to the other points. Now, this question of a buy-back arrangement . . .

Johnson: As you know, our policy is that
after two years we normally sell off our
machinery. But in this particular case,
bearing in mind that these are new
models, I'd like to adopt the policy of
many of your other customers, and have
some form of buy-back arrangement.

Edmonds: Yes. Well, as you know it's not
our normal practice with a plant-hire
company to give a buy-back price – the
reason is obvious. Some of the
machines naturally get a great deal
more wear than others, which is why
you not only maintain such an
up-to-date fleet, but also change your
machines frequently. But we would be
willing to re-purchase the machines on
an independent assessment of their true
market value.

Johnson: Base the buy-back on an
independent assessment?

Edmonds: We pay you whatever
prevailing price an independent assessor
assigns to the machines in two years'
time.

Johnson: I was hoping you'd be able to
give me a guaranteed buy-back price
now – based on a percentage of the
present purchase price.

Edmonds: With inflation the way it is, Mr
Johnson, is that really likely to work out
to more than what the machines'll be
worth in two years from now?

Johnson: Well, how about either a
guaranteed figure now or an
independent valuation in two years' time
– whichever is the greater?

Edmonds: Best of both worlds.

Johnson: You can't whack it, lad.

Edmonds: But there could be a third.
One could envisage a position where an
outside party would buy the machines
from you at a price that's greater than

either the independently assessed
market value, or the price we'd
guarantee you.

Johnson: That's true.

Edmonds: And if these MCMs live up to
their promise it's also slightly more
likely.

Johnson: How about this? You will buy
them back in two years' time at a price
to be arrived at by independent
valuation. But if we can get a better
price than that by selling them off
elsewhere, we remain at liberty to do so.

Edmonds: Yes, we'd be very happy to
agree to that arrangement. Now, you
mentioned training.

Johnson: What I need is a programme
specially for my people, not at your
place, but at our depot in Birmingham
some time in December. Now we will
provide all the facilities, accommodation
and everything else and all you need to
do is to lay on a trainer, all the
necessary aids and a machine for
training and demonstration. That'll save
us both money.

Edmonds: I think that could be difficult.
We wouldn't be able to release the
machine for that long. I'll tell you what.
You want your men on a special course,
without any outsiders. If you could get
your men together over a weekend in
our place instead of Birmingham, I'd
make sure you had the whole of our
training centre to yourselves. Now we'd
provide the machines, lay on everything
else that you need, give them a good
time and generally take care of them.
This way, we wouldn't have to release
that machine out. But do you think you
could get the people to come in?

Johnson: There's no problem in getting
them to come in. But if we do, they are
going to want weekend rates; time and a

Show your research

It helps your credibility to reveal some of your background research, so long as you don't make wrong assumptions or tell the customer his business. But to say to a chain-store manager who may buy your flooring that you've visited a cross-section of his stores to get a better feeling for his needs, will show you are serious, active and determined. He will also have to assume you know more about his business than you perhaps do.

half on Saturday and double time on Sunday. Now, if I have to pay them that kind of money, I imagine that you'd be quite prepared to come to some arrangement about the cost of the training – reducing the course fee per head. Especially since you'll be getting extra mileage out of your centre by opening it at the weekend.

Edmonds: I know what. Instead of Saturday and Sunday, why don't we make it Friday and Saturday? That would reduce your overtime costs by half – and the overtime you do end up paying we could save you by knocking 20 per cent off the training fees.

Johnson: Twenty per cent? Hardly seems enough.

Edmonds: I think it is if you remember that we also wouldn't be passing on to you the extra costs we'd incur by having our staff in on a Saturday.

Johnson: I suppose there is that. Okay, that'd do me on that one.

Edmonds: Good.

Johnson: Which now only leaves us the payment terms to settle. And the more I think about that suggestion of foregoing the 50 per cent deposits in favour of receiving full payment on each machine as soon as it's delivered, the more reasonable it looks to me. After all, Mr Edmonds, I would have thought an order the size I'd placed with you could command some flexibility on your payment policy.

Edmonds: Indeed it does.

Never give a concession, trade it.

Edmonds: But another thought has occurred to me, Mr Johnson. One that perhaps neither of us has been paying enough attention to. These machines

We can give you 2½% on the cheese-and-onion flavour Nibbles if you'll take the black-pudding flavour Scrotlings as well . . .

Never give a concession – trade it.

are a brand-new model, and your company will be the first to use them. In a sense, you'll be our showcase for the MCMs. Now, that being so, I think we've both made a mistake.

Johnson: What mistake have I made?

Edmonds: How important is servicing to you?

Johnson: It's vital. You've no need to sell that to me. You've quoted for it.

Edmonds: Well, the MCMs have been bench-tested, of course, but you and I both know that's not really the same, is it? If anything should go wrong in the field, which your people can't cope with . . .

Johnson: I should expect your people over pretty damn quick.

Edmonds: At weekends? Seven days a week? Day or night? Mr Johnson, that's only on a Grade One level.

Don't go beyond your authority

The urge to complete the sale can stampede you into conceding too much. A buyer may flatter you into feeling that in your position you can extend a discount or credit period. Don't fall for this. In fact it's an easy one to counter: 'I'm authorised to negotiate within the bounds of reason – I could take this one back to Head Ofice but I know they wouldn't wear it. But what if we . . .' – and introduce your own trade-off proposal.

Johnson: But our people asked you for a guaranteed level of technical support on these machines.

Edmonds: But not on a Grade One level. We didn't press it on you, because a Grade One customer is an expensive and time-consuming one for us. But if you're prepared to examine this point in conjunction with the deposit issue, I'll stick my neck out and personally commit my technical services director and his department. I'll have a guarantee of the best Grade One servicing support possible written into the quotation redraft . . .

Johnson: Providing I drop the deposits . . .

Edmonds: Providing that the quotation is agreed in terms of the payment clauses stipulated at present.

Johnson: Have you got the authority to commit a factory head of department?

Edmonds: I'm prepared to lay my neck on the block.

Johnson: It'll be my technical director's neck that's on the block. He should have picked up that one. Right, lad, well I think we've got ourselves a deal. You'll have a glass of whisky?

Edmonds: I certainly will. Water, no ice, please.

Johnson: By the way, you're not looking for a job, are you?

Edmonds: Why?

Johnson: I could use a bright young sales negotiator.

Edmonds: What sort of salary did you have in mind?

Johnson: Subject to negotiation.

Edmonds has done it! He gave nothing away – each time he made a concession he traded something else in exchange, and he has left the client feeling that he too did well out of the negotiation.

Preparation is vital.

Get your customer's total shopping list before you start – and aim high.

Keep the whole package in mind all the time.

Make sure you keep control and set the pace.

Never give a concession – trade it. And make your concessions seem significant.

Keep searching for variables.

Don't make it seem as if you've 'won' a point.

Use the phone or calculator to buy time to think.

Don't exceed your own authority.

Golden rules

8 It's all right, it's only a customer

Reporting to head office

'This is a chore, isn't it? What do they do with all these reports, anyway? Skip them if you can, skimp them if you can't.' So says the old sweat, but don't believe it. Your report reflects yourself and your view of yourself. How many other staff members can advertise themselves to the sales director in a sales-orientated company, or to the managing director, on a regular and frequent basis? It's a wonderful opportunity for the ambitious salesperson who wants to be a high-flyer. But that's not the prime purpose. Your report should enable you to feed back valuable and necessary information for many departments – production, accounts, research and development, as well as sales. That way, it will reflect your awareness and all-round ability at the same time as your call-sheet and order report shows your effectiveness as a salesperson.

Having considered various aspects of the selling process, we are now going to have a look at what can go on at Head Office. Head Office is the natural habitat of Herbert. Every Head Office has got a Herbert or two. Some are infested with them.

Head Office is the nerve centre of the whole organisation. At least, that's what it's supposed to be – the focus of all the information and all the control systems. No wonder Head Offices are such imposing places. You can see them from miles away, like cathedral spires, towering above ordinary mortals, lofty temples of human endeavour. Almost in the clouds – and in Herbert's case you can leave out the 'almost'. But forget the soaring pinnacle for a moment, and look down at the foundations. They're invisible, of course. And so are the foundations of the organisation. Invisible and unspectacular.

Ordinary people – customers, dealers, clients, the public. It's their money that keeps all the Head Office people in business. Their money that pays the wages and salaries and pensions. It's the cash that these people pay out that supports the whole ivory tower. Without it, this busy industrious world would be just a few hundred thousand square feet of empty office space to let with vacant possession.

Head Office doesn't make anything, and it doesn't sell anything. It doesn't normally serve the public directly at all. And to do them justice, most of Herbert's colleagues know it. But they reckon that if they do their job right, everyone else will be able to work better, keeping the foundations strong and sound. But not Herbert . . .

Herbert has drifted away from the real world of customers and costs and profits. He has lost touch with the realities of the market place. Or rather, Head Office has become more important for him than the world outside. He's not just working in it, he's living in it . . . in a world of his own.

Herbert (*to a colleague*): So I said, if they're going to do things prior to obtaining the appropriate authorisations, just because they want something in a hurry and can't be bothered to wait until . . .

Colleague (*sees telephone lying on desk*): I'm in no hurry. Do you want to answer that??

Herbert: It's all right, it's only a customer . . . until such time as we've cleared it against the outstanding accounts file, quite frankly the whole thing is just going to grind to a halt . . .

There's no way of telling a Herbert just by looking at him. The clue is that he doesn't see Head Office's job as supporting everyone else. He sees everyone else's job as supporting Head Office.

Herbert: My word, Maud, listen to this . . . 'Appalling mismanagement . . . contemptible inefficiency . . . arrogant disregard . . .'

Secretary: Who's it from?

Herbert (*scanning*): It's all right, it's only a customer.

The real trouble with Herbert is that the private world of Head Office completely absorbs him. And over the years he's dug a spiritual moat around his castle in the air, and pulled up his mental drawbridge.

The trouble with customers is that most of them live in homes and shops, they run businesses and manage factories. Quite ordinary places. And most of the time they don't encounter Herbert's part of the corporation at all. They deal with the branch offices and area representatives.

Customers in difficulties

As a rep who sells dental requisites, you have a good regular customer. But he's often slow to pay, exceeding his credit limit. Now your Head Office has said you can only sell if payment is made in advance. There are three other suppliers keen to take over, who will give him credit – to start with anyway. What to do? His turnover will be hard to replace. It's a case for negotiation in which you give away nothing but obtain what you need. Use your established relationship – explain the problem. Ask him questions to identify the cause. Then explore solutions. Is he inefficient at accounts? You can personally remind him that your payment is due: collect the cheque if necessary. And remind him that the same situation would recur with another supplier. If he really is bad news, the sooner you know the better, and start looking for sound business elsewhere.

147

But every now and then a customer has to get on to Head Office. And of course he doesn't understand about Herbert and his private world. Not until he's in it, and by then it's too late.

Take Herbert Mark 1, for instance. His private world is made of paper . . .

Herbert (*answering phone*): One moment please.
(*He arranges some papers in the appropriate trays.*)
Orderadmin.
Parker: Pardon?
Herbert: Order Administration.
Parker: Ah yes. I want to know whether I can get A5s with the special optional feature of the C7?
Herbert: Are you internal?
Parker: What does that mean?
Herbert: It means . . . are you in fact internal?
Parker: You mean am I speaking from inside your building? No, I'm not.
Herbert: Ah. So you're external.
(*He picks up the relevant form.*)
Now, could I have that query again, please, and can you tell me the reference number of the PR 17/2?
Parker: I'm afraid I don't know anything about reference numbers. It's the first time I've been on to you.
Herbert: Well, in that case there's not much we can do at this stage.
Parker: At what stage? We aren't at any stage yet.
Herbert: We can't start until a PR 17/2 has been duly raised, you see.
Parker: But can't I just tell you what I want? If I tell you, can't you do the rest?
Herbert: No I can't. It's a physical impossibility.
Parker: It's not a physical impossibility. I am not asking you to defy the Laws of

the Universe. You don't have to levitate slowly from your desk, nor are you required to move backwards in time. All you have to do is take down what I want to buy and ...

Herbert: May I speak frankly? My job is not to sell you things. My job is to process your orders.

Parker: I am placing an order.

Herbert: No you're not. You're telling me you want something.

Parker: Isn't that what placing an order is?

Herbert: I hardly like to state the obvious, sir, but until the PR 17/2 has been raised, duly authorised and properly submitted with copies in triplicate, ordering has definitely occurred.

In the scheme of things your purchase is unimportant, Mr Ackroyd – form along matters, especially form CX531/4.

The Head Office should satisfy customer's needs.

So that's Herbert Mark I. He's lost sight of his organisation's objectives: the forms and procedures and routines started as ways to help achieve the objectives, but for Herbert they've become ends in themselves. A good day's work for him doesn't mean a good day for the organisation. It means a whole lot of forms accurately checked, orders promptly processed and copies correctly filed. He thinks that's what his superiors judge him by.

He doesn't see Head Office as satisfying the customer's needs; he sees the customer as satisfying Head Office's needs.

But there's also Herbert Mark II. His private world is the world of ideas . . .

Herbert (*answering phone*): Hmm?
Parker: Hello, are you Technical Sales??
Herbert: Yes . . . yes . . . we certainly are.
Parker: Well, I wonder if you can tell me whether it's possible to have A5s with the special optional features of the C7?
Herbert: A5s, special optional features C7 . . . What an interesting idea. My word, that is interesting.
Parker: Well, do you think you can do it?
Herbert: Oh, there are some fascinating problems with this one. Oh-ho-ho, now wait a moment . . .
Parker: I'm sorry to interrupt, but is it technically possible or not?
Herbert: Well, technically, of course.
Parker: You can do it?
Herbert: It's technically feasible all right, but you wouldn't want to do it like that.
Parker: Wouldn't it work?
Herbert: It would work all right, but it wouldn't be very elegant, would it?
Parker: Elegant? I want to use it, not wear it. Provided it would actually work, do you think you can at least let me have some information on it?

Herbert: Yes, I think we've got some
chaps who do something like that,
Publications, I think it is. Hang on a
moment (*he juggles with the telephone*) . . .
absolutely fascinating query. Could you
put this through to Sales Pubs, please?

Of course, Herbert Mark II is a very
different character from Herbert Mark I, but
he's just as much of a menace. He's lost sight
of the objectives, too. All that knowledge and
intelligence and expertise are supposed to
help improve the organisation's effectiveness: but for Herbert his knowledge has
become more important than results, and his
experience is more important than service. A
good day's business for him is a day spent
refining his knowledge, even if business has
to wait. Real success isn't a massive order,
it's getting a paper published in a professional journal. Herbert Mark II doesn't see
learning as serving the cause of the organisation, he sees the organisation as serving the
cause of learning.

Then, of course, there's Herbert Mark III.
His private world is the sports and social
club, and he's the life and soul of it . . .

Herbert: And here is the photo of the
chairman's wife opening the new
pavilion – I'll put it here, next to the
account of the last cricket match. So
that's everything except for the
crossword, isn't it?
Secretary: I've spoken to Nick – he's
bringing the crossword over.
Herbert: Well done. Now we can put this
to bed. What's next?
Secretary: The squash draw.
Herbert (*looking at his watch*): Heavens! I
said I'd have it done by lunch.
Secretary: I've got the stuff here.
(*She gives him a box with the tickets in, he
pulls one out.*)

151

Herbert: Well done. Ready? 31 ... 6 ...
(*The phone rings and Herbert answers it.*)
Herbert: Hello. I'm sorry, Jimmy. We're
just doing it now. Be with you in one
second.
Parker: No, this is Frank Parker of
Parker and Gibbs.
Herbert: Sorry, old chap. Sales Pubs
here. What can I do for you? (*he carries
on*) 16 ... 5 ...
Parker: I'm making an enquiry about the
A5.
Herbert (*still drawing numbers*): ... 8 ...
Yes?
Parker: No, not 8, A5.
Herbert: Sorry, old chap, bit chaotic this
end at the moment ... 21 ... just
trying to sort something out.
Parker: I'm interested in A5s with the
optional features of the C7.
Herbert: Ah, that would be a special
order ... 12 ... You don't happen to
have a reference number, do you? Only
it's a bit tricky ...
Secretary: It's the canoe club. They're
cancelling four seats on the Woburn
Abbey trip.
Herbert: Sorry, old chap, just had a bit of
bad news this end. Look, I've just had a
better idea. Why don't you speak to
Order Admin?
Parker: I've been on to them.
Herbert: Oh. Well then, why not have a
word with Technical Sales?
Parker: They put me on to you.
Herbert: Did they? Have you spoken to
Customer Liaison?
Parker: Not yet.
Herbert: Well, they're the ones you want.
Hang on, and I'll have you transferred.

So that's Herbert Mark III. Life and soul of Head Office, another Herbert who's lost sight of his objectives. The house magazine and all those social activities were started because a lot of people work more effectively if they feel they belong to an organisation, instead of just exchanging their labour for money. But when Herbert Mark III gets to work at it, the sports and social activities push the company's objectives into the background. If Herbert Mark III tells you he's done a good day's work you can take it he's completed the tennis tournament, filled up both coaches for the seaside outing, and sold all the tickets for the dance. For him, the organisation is a youth club, with him as the leader. So long as they're all happy playing ping-pong or dancing, he's done his job. He doesn't care if there's no measurable achievement, as long as there's a lot of

It's all right,
it's only a customer

We're poised to become a major UK presence in corporate outings.

Don't lose sight of what Head Office is for.

activity. His ideal customer never bothers
him during office hours, but comes to all the
parties and stays to the end, without ever
spoiling things by trying to talk business.
Herbert Mark III doesn't see social activity
as a good base to build an organisation on –
he sees an organisation as a good base upon
which to build social activity.

So there they are – the three Herberts who
have got so absorbed in their separate Head
Office functions that they've lost sight of
what Head Office is for. They've all changed
it into something else, and by changing it
they're helping to destroy it. Left on their
own, they'd finish it off in a few weeks. But
there are other people in Head Office too –
they're not all Herberts.

Nichols: Peter Nichols speaking,
　　Customer Technical Liaison. Who is
　　that, please?
Parker: Frank Parker of Parker and Gibbs.
Nichols: How can I help you, Mr Parker?
Parker: I'll tell you how you can help me.
　　You can help me by not transferring me
　　to Account Validation so they can put
　　me on to Marketing Anomalies who can
　　refer me to Product Corruption and
　　Perversion, who filed my original letter
　　in the left luggage office at Paddington
　　Station, with my esteemed favour of the
　　14th inst. to hand.
Nichols: I'm not going to transfer you
　　anywhere. My job is to sort out
　　customers' problems, not create them.
　　Now just tell me what you want, and
　　leave the rest to me.
Parker: Just tell you what I want? All
　　right, I want the A5 with the special
　　optional features of a C7.
Nichols: Right.
Parker: Now it's your turn. Whistle and
　　giggle and sing for four minutes, then
　　tell me of course you could do it that

way, but it would be so frightfully
common.

Nichols: I'm sorry, I don't quite follow
you. If the A5 with the C7 features is
what you want, I'll do my best to see
that you get it. So if you'll just supply
the details . . .

Parker: You're trying to trap me, aren't
you? I'm going to have to complete five
copies of 51A and indent on a blue
flimsy to Invoice Section, with two
copies of the counterfoil below the
perforation to Sales Processing.

Nichols: You don't have to fill in any
forms at this stage, Mr Parker.

Parker: No forms? Just tell you what I
want on the phone?

Nichols: That's right. Then I'll find out if
we can manage it and I'll call you back
before three-thirty tomorrow.

Parker: Good Lord.

Nichols: That's all right, isn't it?

Parker: I suppose so. It takes away some
of the sense of achievement. But I don't
really want a sense of achievement. I
simply want an A5 with the special
optional features of the C7.

Nichols: Just one final point, Mr Parker.
Can you tell me why you want that
particular combination?

Parker: Why do you want to know that?
None of the others asked.

Nichols: It's just that if we can't supply
the C7 features with the A5, we might
be able to find another way of helping
you to achieve what you meant.

Parker: It's perfectly simple. The A5 is
basically what I want, but it doesn't
cover the occasional peak volumes I
have to deal with. But there aren't
enough of them to justify the full C7,
and the optional features would be
perfectly adequate if I could get them
with the A5.

Nichols: Mr Parker, I wonder if I could ask you to hold on for a moment, while I fetch some literature.

Parker: Yes, all right. . . . No, it's not all right. He's gone. I knew it. He's gone rock-climbing in his canoe with the rest of the chess club and they won't be back till . . .

Nichols: Sorry to have kept you waiting. Tell me something. Did you consider the B6?

Parker: What's that?

Nicholls: It's just under the A5 in our catalogue. Have you got it in front of you?

Parker: Yes, I have. Oh, here we are. Oh, that's exactly what I want. I wonder how I missed it.

Nichols: Anyway, if that's all right, I'll get on to the branch office, and they'll be round in the morning.

Parker: Fine.

So there we are. By simply bearing in mind that the objective of the company is to sell machinery to customers, Nicholls has been able to solve Parker's problem – which was very simple all along.

That seems a fitting note on which to end our advice on selling. Throughout, we have emphasised the importance of preparation and research, of foreseeing objections and considering how you can overcome them.

Problem-solving for salespeople

We may have our specific problems, but the right technique to use on solving them is the same for salespeople as it is for managing directors or anyone else.

Define the problem
Define what causes it
What ways are there of resolving it?
Compare these ways – which is best?
Decide
Then do it

It's amazing how a simple set of procedures can break down what looked intractable into something that needs only your exercise of will to put into effect. (This last is important. Don't contemplate the solution – do it.)

Don't contemplate the solution – do it!

What all this adds up to is remembering, all the time, that the job is simply to sell – and the best way to guarantee success is not to be born with a silver tongue, but to do your homework and equip yourself with all the information that you are likely to need.

Golden rules

'The customer is always right' – always remember that he is the reason you are in business.

Don't let yourself get so bogged down in paperwork and routine that you lose sight of the company's objectives.

Fulfilling a customer's needs is always more important than refining your own knowledge of a product or technique.

Your company's social club may help its employees to feel happier in their work, but it won't make your customer very happy if it takes precedence over his order.

Remember, your purpose in the company is to sell – so make sure you do it!